ROAD RAGE
TO
ROAD-WISE

ROAD RAGE
TO
ROAD-WISE

THIS BOOK CAN SAVE YOU
OR SOMEONE YOU LOVE

JOHN LARSON, M.D.

with

CAROL RODRIGUEZ, J.D.

FORGE®

A TOM DOHERTY ASSOCIATES BOOK
NEW YORK

ROAD RAGE TO ROAD-WISE

This book is printed on acid-free paper.

A Forge Book
Published by Tom Doherty Associates, Inc.
175 Fifth Avenue
New York, NY 10010

Forge® is a registered trademark of Tom
Doherty Associates, Inc.

Designed by Lisa Pifher

Library of Congress Cataloging-in-
Publication Data
Larson, John A., M.D.
    Road rage to road-wise / John Larson
with Carol Rodriguez.—1st ed.
        p.   cm.
    "A Tom Doherty Associates book."
    ISBN 0-312-89058-3 (alk. paper)
    1. Road rage—United States.   2. Anger—United
States.   3. Aggressiveness (Psychology)—United
States.   4. Automobile drivers—United States—
Psychology.   I. Rodriguez, Carol.   II. Title.
BF575.A5L37   1999
629.28'3'019—dc21   99-21887
                                            CIP

First Edition: June 1999

Printed in the United States of America

0 9 8 7 6 5 4 3 2 1

To my children,
John, Inga, and Chris

CONTENTS

Acknowledgments   9
Foreword by David K. Willis   11
Preface   13

PART ONE:
DEFINING ANGER AND ROAD RAGE:
THE PROBLEM AND THE SOLUTION

1. What Is Road Rage?   23
2. The Relationship Between
   Aggressive Driving and Road Rage   27
3. Larson Driver Stress Profile   31
4. Aggressive Driving and Accidents   37
5. What Causes Anger?   42
6. What Events Make Drivers Angry?   48
7. Dr. Jekyll and Mr. Hyde   57
8. Self-Esteem One Way or Another   66
9. Learning New Beliefs: The Larson
   Driver Attitude Change Seminar   71
10. The Necker Cube's Secret   81
11. Calm Yourself with the Larson
    Driver Relaxation Exercise   87

PART TWO:
THE FIVE STRESSFUL DRIVER BELIEFS
AND HOW TO CHANGE THEM

12. From "Make Good Time" to "Make
    Time Good"   95
13. Installing "Make Time Good"   103
14. From "Be Number One" to "Be a
    Number One Being"   114

15. Installing "Be a Number One Being"   122
16. From "Try and Make Me" to "Be My Guest"   131
17. Installing "Be My Guest"   140
18. From "They Shouldn't Be Allowed" to "Live and Let Live"   150
19. Installing "Live and Let Live"   156
20. From "Teach 'Em A Lesson" to "Leave Punishment to the Police"   164
21. Installing "Leave Punishment to the Police"   170

PART THREE:
THE ROAD TO HEALTH

22. Putting It All Together   185
23. Seat Belts: Why We Don't Wear Them   192
24. When the Other Driver Is Hostile   198
25. Driver Safety Report Cards   210
26. When the Aggressive Driver Is Your Spouse   219
27. Stress Illness: Road Rage and Heart Attacks   227
28. Driving Yourself Healthy   232
29. Driving in Another World   240
30. Measuring Your Change by the Larson Driver Stress Profile   247

ACKNOWLEDGMENTS

I couldn't have written this book without the continued steadfast commitment, love, and support from Patricia MacQueen, my wife and the person who keeps me centered. I cannot say enough about how much my relationship to her has empowered me. Second, my thanks to Herbert Freudenberger, Ph.D., whose wisdom, acquired from surviving the Nazi Holocaust, enabled me to overcome my aversion to taking a stand. Third, my thanks to my children, John, Inga, and Chris, who suffered me through my tempestuous driving years and emerged as wise drivers; and to Leo, Patricia's son, who loves cars and who paid me the highest compliment I could ask for: "You taught me about being a man."

My teacher, Mike Friedman, M.D., made this whole endeavor possible through his brilliant early insights about Type A behavior. I appreciate the confidence he showed in me by allowing part of the Coronary/Cancer Prevention Project to be under my direction at Norwalk Hospital in Connecticut.

This, my second book on aggressive driving and road rage, could not have been written without David Willis, C.E.O. of the AAA Foundation for Traffic Safety, who instantly recognized my first book's merits following my September 1996 presentation at a Washington meeting entitled "Summit to Improve Youthful Driver Performance and Attitude." This was sponsored by State Farm Insurance Companies. Through leadership, and with the help of drivers recruited in June 1997 by the AAA Auto Club of Hartford and the Connecticut AAA Auto Club, I was able to conduct the successful pilot research described in this book.

My gratitude for assisting with that research goes to group leaders Carol Rodriguez, J. D., and Anita Galvan, M.S.W. My appreciation also to Eric and Cathy Trow, who videotaped the entire six-hour seminar and produced a twenty minute video, *Preventing Road Rage: Anger Management for Drivers*, based on this book and marketed through the AAA Foundation for Traffic Safety.

Most especially, though, I want to thank Carol Rodriguez, my colleague and coauthor, for her brilliant insights and ability to reduce forty-five rambling chapters into the thirty much more succinct chapters you'll find here. Writing is rewriting and that takes time, a lot of time. As if in a tennis match, we batted versions of this book back and forth, seeking to return each version received in clearer, cleaner, and more concise language. I didn't write the book; *we* wrote the book.

I also want to thank Rod Rodriguez, J.D., for his generous time and talent in helping prepare the manuscript, and Laura Rodriguez for her administration of the pilot program. I want to acknowledge Jan Mello for typing and retyping the manuscript and Betty Longley for her exceptional organizational skills in running my office, which make it possible for me to work and write.

Stephanie Faul, of the AAA Foundation for Traffic Safety, read earlier versions of the book and made crucial improvements. Heather Wood, my editor at Tor Books, has been simply great to work with. I wish to thank Ginger Clark of Tor books for making everything so easy.

Lastly, my appreciation to all the participants in my seminars through the years who have shared their experiences with me. You'll meet them in the following pages; their stories will show you how to become "Road Wise."

FOREWORD

John Larson has changed the way I drive. I used to be constantly annoyed by the behavior of other drivers, personally offended when cut off in traffic, and quick to lay on the horn or gesture when offended by another "road warrior." Then I read Dr. Larson's first book for angry drivers, *Steering Clear of Highway Madness*.

I've cut my own originally high score on the stress scale featured in this book by more than 50 percent by learning new responses to previously provoking behaviors by other drivers. For example, instead of fuming when cut off by another driver, my usual response today is to take a deep breath and say, "Be my guest!" If you practice this response often enough, it becomes automatic. It is this kind of attitude change that makes Dr. Larson's approach effective.

If you're still skeptical about the value of the anger management techniques you will learn from this book, please skip ahead to chapter 27 ("Stress Illness: Road Rage and Heart Attacks"). It should convince you that following the precepts set forth in the following pages could save your life.

Just one caution, however. Dr. Larson recommends making your car a welcoming environment by carrying along food and beverages and listening to soothing music and books on tape. That's fine, as long as these things don't distract you while driving. Driver inattention is the number one cause of traffic crashes. So, please, don't drink, eat, jot down notes, or talk on your cellular phone while driving—pull over first.

> David K. Willis
> President and Chief Executive Officer
> AAA Foundation for Traffic Safety
> Washington, D.C.

PREFACE

I remember, as a boy in the early 1930s, riding in cars before they had heaters. In the cold Wisconsin winters, we would bundle up and cover our laps with blankets whenever we took a trip. Being on the road was a glorious adventure.

First was the thrill of being transported at speeds not otherwise attainable. Then came the delight of viewing the ever-changing panorama on both sides of the car. How interesting to see such diversity of beauty! I never knew what to expect.

It was fun anticipating our arrival at familiar destinations—Grandmother's farm, Taylor's Falls, Balsam Lake—and visiting with "distant" relatives who lived in St. Paul, Minnesota, 36 miles away. I felt special when my father took me along while he visited area farmers to whom he sold machinery. I'll always remember him singing "Moonlight Bay," "Sweet Adeline," "My Wild Irish Rose," and other tunes on the way home.

Of course, the unexpected often happened: flat tires; getting stuck in snow; pulling through the muddy ruts of new construction; encounters with chickens, cows, hay wagons, horses, and billows of dust from passing cars, all of which presented ordinary hazards.

But while being on the road was a joy to me, it was often stressful to my father. When traveling long distances he was obsessed with "making good time," and he set daily mileage goals that strained the endurance of his children, not to mention his patient wife. My father battled other cars to reach his goals, creating tension and irritation. He turned what should have been an adventurous, joyful journey into an anxiety-filled competition.

When I began driving—an activity I love—I drove like my dad: fast, setting rigorous driving goals; and I became furious at the "stupidity" of some drivers.

I never thought there was anything wrong with my attitude. Later, during my psychiatric residency at the Menninger Clinic, interested in what was then called psychosomatic medicine, I discovered that attitudes affect health. I particularly admired the theories of Franz Alexander, a Chicago psychoanalyst, who suggested that emotional states cause illness.

In 1963, while chief of psychiatry at Springfield Hospital in Springfield, Massachusetts, I was asked to consult on the case of a thirty-four-year old insurance salesman who had had a heart attack. He had stressed himself with his bottled-up anger, his ferocious striving, and his hectic pace. Though at the time I did not question him about his driving habits, I have no doubt—judging from my experience treating more than a thousand people with heart attacks—that he "battled" traffic much as my father did.

Alexander's theories about the role of the psyche in heart attacks began to make more sense. From that day, over thirty years ago, until this moment, the prevention of heart attacks by psychological intervention has been my primary professional interest.

Concurrently with my meeting that salesman, two cardiologists in San Francisco, Dr. Meyer Friedman and Dr. Raymond Rosenman, were conducting research that was to prove a strong link between Type A men—those quick to get angry, irritated, aggravated, or impatient at the slightest provocation (including highway frustrations)—and their propensity for heart attack.

Since 1984, after having learned successful behavior modification techniques at the Friedman Institute, I have treated coronary-prone individuals at the Institute of Stress Medicine at Norwalk Hospital, in Norwalk, Connecticut. My studies have taught me that men and women who have had heart attacks tend to overreact to events that happen while they're driving. In group treatment, this overreaction to highway stressors becomes the focus for behavioral change. Cognitive therapy treatment techniques, like those described in this book, have been applied with considerable success. Patients become calmer, less angry drivers.

In the process of helping my patients prevent heart attacks, I have become knowledgeable about highway stress in general, and, most important, how to reduce it.

This book is intended to enable you to change those attitudes that may cause you to overreact to highway stressors. When you alter these attitudes and beliefs, you lower the duration, frequency, and intensity of your tension while you are driving. As your stress reaction lowers, so will the chances of your having a heart attack or suffering other stress-related illnesses.

Soon after the publication of my first book on this topic, *Steering Clear of Highway Madness*, in July 1996, a research group under Louis Mizell completed its survey of "road rage" incidents as recorded in the nation's newspapers from September 1990 to September 1996. This report, released later in the year by the AAA Foundation for Traffic Safety, which had underwritten the survey, revealed a 51 percent increase in the number of assaults reported annually during that period, with a

total of 10,037 incidents of violence between drivers, including 218 deaths and 12,610 injuries.

In September 1996, I met David Willis, presi-
dent of the AAA Foundation for Traffic Safety, in
Washington at a "Safety Summit" meeting sponsored by the State Farm Insurance Company. He
read my book, found the hypothesis convincing, and
invited me to speak at the foundation's annual Research and Development Committee meeting in
February 1997. As a result of that meeting, the
board of directors authorized funding for a pilot research study based on the treatment of road rage
and aggressive driving described in the book.

The resulting six-hour seminar, titled "Controlling Aggressive Driving: Yours and Theirs," was
conducted in June 1997 with aggressive drivers recruited by the two Connecticut AAA motor clubs.
Evaluations of the results were made at a second
meeting held in September 1997. The results confirmed the book's hypothesis: all but one of the fifteen most aggressive drivers reported a 50 percent
drop in the frequency of their aggressive driving
behavior and in the intensity of their anger. They
no longer became enraged while driving.

The year 1997 also witnessed a media preoccupation with road rage. All the major television
networks devoted hour-long programs to the phenomenon. News media, including newspapers, radio,
and television, reported the frequent occurrence of
violence between drivers. A simple search of the In-
ternet produced *over eight thousand* mentions of the
term "road rage." Polls indicated that 50 percent of
all motorists feared aggressive drivers. The reason
for this became clear: violence between drivers
had not been the only consequence of aggressive
driving habits. Dr. Ricardo Martinez, director of
the National Highway Traffic Safety Administration (NHTSA), announced that two-thirds of high-

way deaths were caused by behavior associated with aggressive driving. Small wonder at the national interest.

For me, the time since the first book's publication has brought a flood of questions and comments from legions of reporters writing articles, as well as from participants in seminars, and from audiences I have addressed. I've learned from them and from the research I and my colleagues, Carol Rodriguez and Anita Galvan, conducted. Therefore, after conferences with Stephanie Faul and David Willis of the AAA Foundation for Traffic Safety, likewise besieged with questions about the cause and treatment of road rage and aggressive driving, I concluded that a second book incorporating the new data should be written.

Readers of the first book will find that, though the basic hypothesis remains intact, its presentation has been changed in many respects for this second work.

This book is for all road users, drivers and passengers alike. Readers who don't suffer from road rage, or who only get cross and irritable when they experience provocative driving behavior in other drivers, will learn strategies to follow to avoid trouble on the road. Passengers can develop techniques for defusing potentially dangerous situations. And for those who *do* suffer from road rage, in all its manifestations, the treatment approaches described may well prove lifesaving.

This book is meant as a treatment book. Anyone who reads and understands it and does the exercises should experience less anger while driving. Since repetition and reinforcement are necessary for learning, words and phrases are repeated and paraphrased throughout the text.

In order to gauge how well this works, I urge you to complete the Larson Driver Stress Profile in chapter 3. Be honest with your answers. Then, after reading the book, doing the exercises, and practicing on the road for one month, retake the test as shown again in chapter 30 without looking at your previous results. Be honest at this point, too. Three months after reading this book, you should see further improvement.

I believe you will find that your highway anger is reduced, your driving safety enhanced, and your enjoyment of your journeys on the road increased.

ROAD RAGE
TO
ROAD-WISE

PART ONE

DEFINING ANGER AND ROAD RAGE:
THE PROBLEM AND THE SOLUTION

Donald Graham, a fifty-four-year-old church deacon, was driving home with his wife after an afternoon of square dancing when he saw a car using high beams to tailgate another. He decided that wasn't right, and took it upon himself to teach the tailgater a lesson by giving him a taste of his own medicine.

Graham then tailgated the tailgater, using bright beams, too. No matter how fast or slow the other driver (Michael Blodgett, forty-two, an emergency-room technician) drove, Graham stayed right behind him. Even when Blodgett moved into the middle lane, Graham stuck to him like glue.

Finally Blodgett pulled over to the side, and the deacon did the same, a short distance behind. Blodgett and his male passenger got out and proceeded to walk toward the deacon's car. Expecting to find a formidable foe, one of the men carried a long, heavy-duty flashlight. The deacon, seeing the two men approaching, decided they were as malevolent as he had originally suspected. He took a crossbow out of his trunk, loaded a hunting arrow, and fired. Saying "He shot me," Blodgett fell, mortally wounded; he died before he reached the hospital.

Even after going to prison, Donald Graham stoutly maintained that he had acted only in self-defense.

HIGHWAY HOSTILITY WIDESPREAD

Incidents of drivers physically assaulting other drivers on U.S. highways were first reported in

1978, in the *Wall Street Journal*. By 1981, such incidents had increased. The *New York Times* described violence in Houston, where twelve traffic-related homicides occurred in one year. One Texas state trooper dubbed the phenomenon "unfriendly driving."

These incidents continued in Houston for some time; during one ten-month period there were 161 formal complaints of violent altercations, from fist-fights to fatal shootings, as a result of driving frustration.

Houston was not alone. Other major cities have witnessed similar highway violence. During the summer of 1987, the *Journal of the American Medical Association* published a study documenting 137 incidents of highway assault with firearms in Los Angeles County. Eighty-three shootings occurred, resulting in seventeen injuries, including two fatalities. The highway events triggering the confrontations were lane-changing, merging, tailgating, speeding, and impeding traffic.

Nor do Texas and California drivers have a monopoly on highway mayhem. Weapons and violence are just as visible in Detroit, where, during a four-month period, twenty-eight shootings were reported.

An Illinois state highway patrol officer reports receiving two or three calls each day about altercations between motorists. State trooper Ty Kansaki comments: "The most minor traffic accident leads people to slug it out." Kansaki has avowed that he will no longer go on patrol without his bulletproof vest. "We're just trying to keep them from hurting and killing each other," he says.

In Louisiana, state trooper Mike Taylor characterizes altercations between motorists as "the Jekyll-and-Hyde syndrome." According to Taylor, otherwise normal citizens are losing their heads over minor blacktop annoyances. "People who get caught up in these incidents seem to go nuts," he says. "But, in sixteen years on the job, I've found that if a guy is overly emotional and extremely upset, once you get him out of the car he calms down."

In Denver, the statistics on road rage indicate that Rocky Mountain drivers are not immune to the highway hostility virus: during a three-year period, four motorists were shot to death and six seriously injured after traffic altercations. "We know it wasn't summer that did it—the heat and temperature and all—because a lot of it was in the winter" said Denver police detective John Wyckoff.

In San Francisco, at least seven violent incidents among drivers, including one death, happened within one month. Three occurred on the Bay Bridge, a bumper-to-bumper span between San Francisco and Oakland, and three others took place near San Francisco International Airport when repaving operations snarled traffic and elevated tempers.

In Portland, 600 miles north, between November and February, 1993, police received more than sixty reports of projectiles smashing into car windows. One man was charged with attempted murder when he allegedly shot a bullet through the window of a taxicab.

In 1988, a story in a Florida newspaper, describing similar happenings, used the term "road rage" to identify such out-of-control violence. The term stuck.

In 1997, Louis Mizell undertook a six-year compilation of newspaper stories on highway violence, underwritten by the AAA Foundation for Traffic Safety. Between September 1, 1990, and September 1, 1996, he documented a 51 percent increase in the reporting of such occurrences. In all, there were 10,037 assaults reported, including 218 murders and 12,610 injuries. As in the study published in the *Journal of the American Medical Association*, the traffic circumstances that most commonly gave rise to the violence were tailgating, lane-changing (cutting off), speeding, impeding traffic (failure to yield right of way), and merging.

Violence alarms us. When it occurs it makes newspaper headlines, and it is widely broadcast over television and radio. And for good reason: we want to know where danger lurks so we can protect ourselves. But violence alone doesn't account for the enormous public concern. That concern was there long before the Mizell report. However, there is no doubt that this AAA Foundation–sponsored study sparked the long-overdue public outcry.

Since I began speaking on highway violence in 1988, audiences have come alive when I discussed what I then called "overreactive anger." At parties, it seemed almost everyone had a war story to tell about some angry exchange with another driver. People were in a furor over the pervasive meanness, hostility, and ugly finger-raising, face-making, and name-calling rampant among American drivers.

Road rage incidents, where actual physical assaults take place, are only the tip of the iceberg. Lesser forms of assault, including ugly, threatening gestures, verbal attacks, and using one's automobile to harass other drivers, are endemic. If looks could kill, there would be widespread slaughter.

We Americans often behave despicably in our automobiles. With astounding frequency, Americans experience the urge to harm or kill while driving. Such levels of anger would never occur between the same individuals were they to meet on the street, even if one person inadvertently bumped into the other.

This anger is a direct consequence of aggressive driving. Anger while driving and road rage would not occur without aggressive driving.

What exactly is aggressive driving and how does it result in anger and road rage?

I define an aggressive driver as a driver who, in his determination to achieve certain goals, engages in risky driving behaviors—speeding, competing, tailgating, cutting off, refusal to yield right of way, weaving, lane changing without signaling, running red lights, making illegal turns—and is inconsiderate of other drivers and of passengers.

The Maryland State Police have a shorter working definition: "A driver who operates his vehicle in a bold and pushy manner, endangering the lives and property of other motorists."

There is a sequence of escalating abuse of one driver by another. The first step is a single gesture, curse, or grimace delivered as retaliation. The second step is vigilante behavior: when the aggressive driver encounters another vehicle that inadvertently impedes or thwarts his aggressive driving, he punishes the other driver by scornful, hateful looks, curses, and obscene gestures. The third step is when the vigilante, in response to some form of retaliation by the driver he has punished, escalates his abuse of the other driver by harassing him with closer tailgating, bright lights, braking suddenly while traveling in front of him, or driving excessively slowly.

Road rage is the fourth step, where the vigilante further escalates abuse and punishment of another combative driver by seeking to physically injure the other driver's vehicle, person, or passengers.

And don't think that the anger is limited to men. This is no longer true, especially on the road. A study of drivers in Michigan, conducted during the summer of 1997 by the Michigan State Police using a modified version of the Larson Driver Stress Profile, revealed that reported anger among young women drivers was slightly higher than among young men.

So what is the result of all this anger on the road? Violence, accidents, and stress illness. At first glance these three phenomena may seem to be quite different, but more than thirty years of studying stress convinces me they are linked by emotional states growing out of five common attitudes or beliefs present to various degrees in all drivers.

Evidence shows that when these attitudes are challenged by frustrating highway events, strong emotional states characterized by anxiety, impatience, resentment, anger, and rage are triggered. Like water heated to the boiling point, flaring emotions can overwhelm the driver's judgment, leading to violence and risky driving behaviors. When they become chronic and repetitive, these emotions can bring about pathological changes within the driver's body. The result is disease, in addition to the increased risk of accidents, injuries, and death.

Feelings of intense anger and rage triggered by either another driver's behavior or a road condition can lead to periods of irrational thoughts, feelings, and behavior that last from seconds to hours. During this period, a driver:

1. Experiences exaggerated anger, irritation, aggravation, and impatience focusing on the most trivial occurrences;

2. Becomes preoccupied with thoughts about what happened and distracted from concentrating on driving, thus becoming vulnerable to new danger;

3. Forms irrational convictions about the personality and motivations of the other driver, based on flimsy evidence;

4. Experiences impaired judgment, saying or doing things he or she later regrets, including engaging in risky driving behavior while attempting to punish or retaliate against the offending driver;

5. Suffers from diminished sensibilities— i.e., the ability to hear, see, feel, touch, smell, and taste is dulled.

6. Loses brain capacity, the power of abstract thinking, empathy, humor, appreciation of beauty, and the ability to feel love.

If we understand the mental mechanisms involved in the chain of events leading to hostile driver behavior, prevention of many highway calamities becomes possible. Unquestionably, as our nation's roads become more crowded with impatient drivers jostling for space and advantage, angry encounters will become more common and more deadly. We must find a new way of thinking.

Every driver has the ability to change his or her attitudes without any negative effect on driving or arrival time. With the change in perception that develops from these new driving attitudes comes a new joy behind the wheel and a sense of freedom and satisfaction the driver may have thought lost. Not only driving will be more relaxed, enjoyable, and free of hostility, but the chance of accidents will be significantly reduced.

To convince you that what I'm suggesting is practical, very "doable" for the average driver (not to mention the fact that it may save your life!), I wish, first, to make you better acquainted with how to measure your own highway hostility. Then we'll start our journey of prevention by examining the different attitudes that motivate pugnacious driving and move on to the simple but effective methods that can alter these destructive attitudes permanently.

That our highways have become uncertain and dangerous is not news. I should know, for even though I am a physician and an expert in stress medicine, I was an angry driver before I discovered the harm I was doing to myself and the high risk of traffic mayhem I was contributing to by my get-out-of-my-way attitude. And I was not alone.

Before starting on this journey, take the following test to determine your current level of highway stress. Be honest; that way you can see for yourself just how much the information contained in this book really helps to make your driving less stressful and more pleasurable. One month after reading the book, memorizing the new beliefs, and practicing, take the test again. (There's another copy in chapter 30). I can guarantee that if you've finished those three steps, your stress scores will be dramatically reduced. Please take the test now.

Score each statement as follows:

3   If it's true for you, even for a moment, almost every time your drive

2   If it's true for you, even for a moment, often when you drive

1   If it's true for you only once in a while

0   If it's never true for you

Larson Driver Stress Profile

I. Anger

1. Get angry at drivers _____
2. Get angry at fast drivers _____
3. Get angry at slow drivers _____
4. Get angry when cut off _____
5. Get angry at malfunctioning stoplights _____
6. Get angry at traffic jams _____
7. Spouse or friends tell you to calm down _____
8. Get angry at tailgaters _____
9. Get angry at your passengers _____
10. Get angry when a multilane highway narrows _____
    Total I _____

II. Impatience

1. Impatient waiting for passengers to get in _____
2. Impatient in traffic jams _____
3. Impatient at stoplights _____
4. Impatient waiting in lines (car wash, bank) _____
5. Impatient waiting for parking space _____
6. As passenger, impatient with driver _____
7. Impatient when car ahead slows down _____
8. Impatient if behind schedule on a trip _____
9. Impatient driving in far right, slow lane _____
10. Impatient with pedestrians crossing street _____
    Total II _____

III. Competing

1. Compete with another car _____
2. Compete with yourself (to break travel time, etc.) _____
3. Personalize the competition with another driver _____
4. Challenge other drivers (initiate the competition) _____

5. Race other drivers on thruways _____
6. Compete with cars in tollbooth lines _____
7. Compete with cars in traffic jams _____
   (to move up faster)
8. Compete with drivers who challenge you _____
9. Compete with yourself or others to amuse _____
   yourself when bored
10. Drag-race adjacent car at stoplights _____
    Total III _____

IV. Punishing ("Teach them a lesson," "Pay them back.")

1. "Punish" bad drivers _____
2. Complain to passengers about other drivers _____
3. Curse at other drivers _____
4. Make obscene gestures _____
5. Block tailgaters who want to pass _____
6. Block cars trying to change lanes _____
7. Tailgate cars that won't yield to you _____
8. Brake suddenly to send a message to tailgater _____
9. Use high beams to punish drivers who won't _____
   pull over
10. Seek to damage another's car or person _____
    Total IV _____

    Total of I, II, III, IV _____

Answering honestly and accurately, you can obtain a measure of your hostility on the road. Since we tend to underestimate our reactivity, it may help to take this with a friend or spouse, asking him or her to check your answers for accuracy and honesty.

Significance of your score:

I. Anger   (possible score: 30)
   High   9+
   Moderate   5–8
   Low   0–4

II.	Impatience	(possible score: 30)
	High	9+
	Moderate	5–8
	Low	0–4

III.	Competing	(possible score: 30)
	High	9+
	Moderate	5–8
	Low	0–4

IV.	Punishing	(possible score: 30)
	High	9+
	Moderate	5–8
	Low	0–4

Total	(possible score: 120)
High	35+
Moderate	16–34
Low	0–15

HIGH SCORER: If your score was thirty-five or above, then you are very likely to be involved in a road rage incident. High scorers get angry at other drivers almost every time they get in a car, even as a passenger. Take a look at your scores on each of the four sections. Notice how you scored on the "Competing" and "Punishing" sections. If you scored over nine on either or both of those sections, then you're especially at risk. It would be a good idea for you to read this book carefully, following all the exercises, or enroll in a Larson Driver Attitude Change Seminar—or both! Not only are you at risk of accident-related injury or death, but you are also increasing your chances of a heart attack if you keep it up.

The good news for you is that at least you're honest, and aware of how you're feeling, so you're

LARSON DRIVER STRESS PROFILE

at a good starting point. (Some people will deny their anger, or be so uninvolved in the test that they score low even though they are very aggressive drivers.) The even better news for you is that the most aggressive drivers experience the most change after reading the book. Driving can be a source of tremendous pleasure for you. So read on!

MODERATE SCORER: If you scored between sixteen and thirty-four, you scored in the moderate range. You often get angry at other drivers, but you also enjoy your ride some of the time. If you scored at the higher end of the moderate scale, you may actually be a very aggressive driver, depending on how honest you were with yourself when you answered the questions. Some very aggressive drivers have scored in the moderate range. Go back and reconsider your answers carefully. Pay particular attention to your scores for the "Competing" and "Punishing" sections. If you scored nine or over on either or both of those sections, you are an aggressive driver, even if your scores on the first two sections were low.

If you answered as honestly as you could, and a close friend or spouse agrees with your answers, you truly are a moderately angry driver. The good news for you is that the more aggressive you are now, the more you'll appreciate the changes you'll make after carefully reading this book and following all the exercises. You won't believe how pleasurable driving can be. Read on!

LOW SCORER: If you scored between zero and fifteen, then you are a calm driver. You are at the lowest risk of an injury or accident due to road rage since you don't get aggravated easily and you don't punish other drivers. You don't feel like punishing them because they didn't make you angry in the first place! You are also probably at the lowest risk, among drivers, of a heart attack or other stress-related illness. Congratulations! But don't stop reading yet. This book could still be very helpful to you in understanding what makes aggressive drivers angry so you can stay off their enemy list.

Since most individuals do answer honestly, the Larson Driver Stress Profile is an accurate instrument through which we can determine who the high-risk drivers are. If we had a method to reduce those high-risk scores, thousands could be saved from death and injury. Health care costs could be reduced by millions.

Luckily, we do have such a treatment approach. To understand how it works, you must know more about how anger comes about, and how it can be reduced.

"I didn't see him coming." Police hear this most often as the reason for an accident. We all know that when we become furious, our judgment becomes impaired: we will do and say things we later regret. When this happens while driving, particularly at high speeds, our anger distracts us from paying full attention. It takes only seconds of distraction to go off the road, slam into the car that unexpectedly stops in front of us, move into the adjoining lane and strike the car traveling there, or go through a stop sign that was partially obscured.

When I think back on the several fender benders I've had during fifty years of driving, all came as the results of impatience and not paying full attention to where I was going. Fortunately, I've had no major accidents due to this behavior. But others have not been so lucky.

Automobile accidents occur frequently in all parts of the United States and around the world. London gets the title for being the first city with a fatal accident. It happened in August 1896, at the Crystal Palace in South London: Bridget Driscoll became the first victim of a car accident, as reported by Peter Marsh and Peter Collett in their book *Driving Passion: The Psychology of the Car*. Three years later, Henry Bliss became the first to suffer the same fate in the United States.

In 1951, Elma Wischmeier became the millionth American killed on the road. By 1986, the fatality rate had climbed so high that a record 37 people in the United States died each year for every 100,000 cars on the road. In Belgium and Germany, the figure is four times as high. Israel and Greece have the highest auto fatality rate in the world: 200 and 195 deaths, respectively, per 100,000 vehicles.

Giving greater meaning to those statistics, an article in the *Journal of the American Medical Association* reported in September 1994 that 6,000 persons aged sixteen to twenty died from motor vehicle crashes in 1991, twice as many as from any other cause of death among persons in this age group.

The same *JAMA* article observed: "Young drivers account disproportionately for motor vehicle crashes worldwide, reflecting, in part, the combination of immaturity and lack of driving experience. Adolescent drivers are more apt than adult drivers to resort to speeding, running red lights, making illegal turns, not wearing safety belts, riding with an intoxicated driver, and driving after using drugs and alcohol."

The need to modify drivers'. attitudes, both nationally and internationally, was demonstrated by a report on Portugal that appeared in the *New York Times* in May, 1991. "Driving is Portugal's number one public health problem," Major Gabriel Mendes, the deputy commander of the country's Transit Brigade, is quoted as saying. "People behave very differently when they are in the driver's seat from what they do in ordinary life.

"The Portuguese have the reputation of being a quiet, law-abiding and introverted people, who, even in times of political turmoil, go out of their way to avoid using violence. But, mysteriously, when they get into their cars, they are aggressive and dangerous."

"In Lisbon, they careen up and down the city's steep hills, immune to the presence of pedestrians or other drivers. Outside the capital, their specialty seems to be overtaking on blind corners, a problem aggravated by the fact that the country still has only 200 miles of modern highways. The death rate on Portugal's roads is consistently the highest within the 12-nation European Community. Measured in relation to total vehicles, it is four times higher than Britain, the Netherlands, and the United States."

There is a similar problem in Sweden, according to Professor Ray Fuller of the University of Dublin. "A Swedish study of speeds on narrow winding roadways showed that drivers ultimately learn to travel at such a speed that, should an obstruction occur around the next bend, they would have no chance of avoiding a collision. Such behavioral traps arise," he said, "because the connection between a particularly rewarding driving behavior (traveling at high speed) and a hazardous consequence is improbable and uncertain." In other words, since nothing, probably, will go wrong, why not enjoy the speed?

In the United States the stories keep pouring in.

On April 17, 1997, two young men, Narkey Keval Terry and Billy Canipe, both twenty-six years old, raced each other for fifteen minutes during morning rush hour at 80 mph on the George Washington Memorial Parkway in McLean, Virginia. Terry's Jeep struck the rear of Canipe's car, sending it out of control across the median, where it struck two other cars, killing Canipe and the two other, completely innocent, drivers. Terry was convicted of manslaughter and sentenced to thirteen years in prison.

Yet there are those who deny that road rage is a problem. A November 1998 *Washington Post* story, "A Crises That May Not Exist Is All the Rage," blames road rage all on "media frenzy." The authors write, "Examples of true [?] road rage—such as the driving duel that resulted in three deaths on the George Washington Parkway—remain exceedingly rare."

The authors gave no examples of what "false" road rage would look like. If "true" road rage means two drivers who intentionally try to harm each other, Mizell found "only" 218 deaths and 10,000 injuries due to overt attacks. But that is only the tip of the iceberg of the aggressive road-rage driving phenomenon.

Rage short of physical violence abounds on our highways. Thirty percent of the members of any audience I've spoken to since 1988 say they've had the "urge to kill" while driving and 70 percent report being threatened or harassed by an angry driver within the previous two weeks. Most readers of this book will recall seeing an outraged driver within the past month.

In addition to the hostility there are deaths, over 25,000 a year, according to Dr. Ricardo Martinez of the National Highway Traffic Safety Administration, who has estimated that two-thirds of all traffic fatalities occurred in accidents where overly aggressive driving played a major role. Most accidents are not accidental! The same aggressive driving that gives rise to 218 "road rage" deaths in six years also accounts for more than 25,000 deaths annually from traffic accidents. That also translates into being responsible for 4 million of the 6 million motor vehicle crashes; 2 million of the 3 million injuries; and 80 billion of the 120 billion annual societal costs.

How can we reduce this overwhelming human suffering and financial loss? If we could identify these aggressive drivers and change their attitudes about driving, we could dramatically reduce the tremendous toll their driving takes on society. In order to understand why these high scorers take the daily risks they do, we have to understand their anger.

In Houston, Allen Wilder's car stalled in the middle of a jammed freeway. He couldn't get it started. Behind him, the driver of a dump truck became aggravated and rammed Wilder viciously. Then, still steaming, the driver jumped out of the truck with a steel bolt and began to beat on the trunk of Wilder's car. When Wilder tried to stop the mayhem, the truck driver struck his forearm, breaking it, then drove off when another driver yelled at him.

Anger arises when your beliefs are challenged. So what could the dump truck driver possibly have believed that would make him lose control? Probably something like "No one should stop in the middle of the road" or "No one blocks me and gets away with it." Maybe he thought Wilder stopped on purpose just to annoy him or that Wilder wasn't paying attention to the road, thus holding him up. Once the dump truck driver had concluded that Wilder was doing something wrong that delayed him, he became enraged and proceeded to punish Wilder for challenging his belief that "No one blocks me."

We each define rules of the road for our own and other drivers' behavior—rules that we believe in strongly and are willing to defend. When other drivers challenge our rules, as they will almost every day, we get angry. If you believe drivers should drive within posted speed limits, you'll become angry if someone goes faster. If you believe that under no circumstances should anyone cut you off, you'll become angry when that happens. In order to understand our anger, we need to identify

our beliefs and learn alternative beliefs and attitudes toward other drivers that are less likely to set
us up for angry reactions.

There are five key beliefs that determine nearly all
anger on the road. The driver who does not hold to
these beliefs scores in the low range of the Larson
Driver Stress Profile, and will never experience
road rage. The driver who holds to all five beliefs
will score over thirty-five on the Larson Driver
Stress Profile and will have at least short episodes
of fury every time he or she drives. And if this
driver has an encounter with another like-minded
driver, the fury could escalate into road rage—driving erratically and seeking to harm the other driver
in some way to "make him pay."

Belief #1: "Make Good Time"

The person holding this belief feels that he or she
should drive to his or her destination as fast as possible within a certain self-prescribed amount of
time. Anger results when the rate of speed or time
schedule cannot be achieved. Whoever or whatever
is deemed responsible for bringing about the delay
becomes the object of rage. A person making a
wrong turn, a slow-moving pedestrian in a crosswalk, a stalled vehicle blocking the lane, road construction, an unexpected stop sign, or a traffic jam
can easily bring on rage.

Belief #2: "Be Number One"

Being number one is a national obsession. Extended
to the road, this belief holds that the way to gain

self-esteem and status is to beat the driver of another car in some self-created contest. Anger results when the other driver appears to be winning
or actually does win the contest. The "contest" may
be a race at high speed, or a question of who merges
ahead of whom, or who gets through a tollbooth line
first, or which lane moves faster in a traffic jam.

Belief #3: "Try and Make Me"

This belief holds that "I may not win, but I'm sure
not going to lose." There is a perception that self-
esteem is lost by giving in and allowing a demand-
ing driver to have his way. Anger results when the
other driver persists, escalates his efforts, or actually succeeds in achieving his objective. That objective may be to pass, drive faster, merge, go slow,
or cut in.

Belief #4: "They Shouldn't Be Allowed"

This belief holds that any driver, vehicle, driving
behavior, or highway activity that fails to measure
up to this driver's self-created, unrelenting standard should be banned from the road he or she oc-
cupies.

Anger results whenever this driver observes an
"infraction" of his or her standard. Common elements that conflict with these arbitrary standards
may include speed, gender of driver, lane changing,
make of car, automobile decorations, age of driver,
attitude of other driver, or the consequences of
highway construction.

Belief #5: "Teach 'em a Lesson"

The driver who acts as policeman, judge, and jury believes that he or she has the right to punish other drivers whose motoring threatens, annoys, inconveniences, or fails to measure up to his or her self-created standards.

Anger, already present in this belief holder, escalates when an infraction occurs and peaks as he or she delivers punishment. Punishment may consist of swearing, making obscene gestures, pounding on the wheel or dash, scowling, shouting obscenities, blocking an offending vehicle, running the other vehicle off the road, or even killing the other driver.

As you can see, the anger is never due to the event itself; its occurrence depends upon the context within which the event takes place and the meaning of the event to the individual. The beliefs we hold create the context within which we live. These five beliefs are each wedded to the driver's sense of what makes up his or her "self," just as the driver's right arm is part of his or her "self." Our sense of self is more than our bodies; it encompasses certain heartfelt beliefs that cannot be transgressed without destroying some of one's self. A driver will fight, drive recklessly, and sometimes even kill to defend them.

Take General Custer as an example from history. He prided himself on his daring, his risk-taking, and a heroic sense of self that he believed would lead him to greatness and a political career. Prior to the Battle of Little Big Horn his Indian scouts warned him of the size of the Indian encampment. However, his own concept of a self that could always prevail led him to divide up his already too-small force into three weaker groups in order to surround the Indians and prevent their escape.

At some point as he galloped forward in the attack, it must have dawned on him that the foe vastly outnumbered his small force. To retreat, however, would mean the death of his self-concept, "the risk-taking victorious hero." He chose to hold on to his belief even though it meant the death of his biological self. And, indeed, he is still remembered as a dashing hero: his psychological self lives on in our minds.

I am convinced that this phenomenon happens over and over again every day to drivers wedded to their beliefs. My experience in treating aggressive drivers gives me countless illustrations of the willingness to risk a real injury, illness, or death in order to avoid a psychological death.

That is why all anger on the road is experienced as righteous indignation. Drivers with road rage feel aggrieved and are impelled to redress the injustice. They feel like victims, as if they are being unfairly punished for trying to correct what they perceive to be morally wrong. Anger is the body's signal that something has gone wrong in our world, and that some person is responsible. We don't get angry at events that we can't hold anyone responsible for. An unexpected shower spoiling our picnic is disappointing, but we don't feel anger (unless we hold God responsible, or the person who insisted on having the picnic today instead of yesterday, when it was sunny).

If you believe that slow drivers in the far left lane should pull over and let you pass when you flash your lights, signaling your desire, and they don't, you'll feel some degree of annoyance or anger.

The violation of our beliefs feels personal, even though we know intellectually that it isn't. That's because our beliefs are personal, and we experience the violation as a personal challenge.

Even something as minor as someone calling us by the wrong name can make us angry. We'll experience some degree of annoyance until we set the matter straight. Viewed in this way, anger has a constructive purpose: it alerts us to something amiss in our world. It's a vital part of the human brain's signaling mechanism, telling us that someone threatens our self-interest—threatens what we believe in.

Anger not only signals a threat, but it denotes the existence of an energy that empowers us to take action to put things back in order, our order.

Now let's take a look at what makes drivers angry.

The dusk and mist made visibility poor as my friend Frank drove us toward the Norwalk, Connecticut, YMCA for our weekly racquetball game. We were chatting amiably, when we suddenly noticed a stalled car looming dead ahead in the far right lane of a four-lane street.

Frank instinctively veered left, but braked hard when a pickup truck, already traveling there, blocked the lane change. After holding up momentarily, Frank fell in behind the truck, and we resumed our conversation, thinking nothing of the incident.

A block later, we stopped behind the truck at a stoplight. Frank flashed his left-turn indicator. We continued talking and didn't notice for several moments that the light had changed. The truck hadn't moved. It took us a few seconds to determine that the truck's driver was punishing us for having come too close to him.

There was sufficient room to turn left behind the truck, but when Frank did this, the truck's driver wheeled his vehicle sharply in an attempt to beat us around the corner. He failed and we were ahead of him. A half block later, as we slowed to turn into the YMCA, he roared past, determined to beat us to the next stoplight, which he thought was our destination.

"He's crazy," Frank said. We both assumed the truck driver, having experienced his little victory, would be satisfied, but we were wrong.

As we prepared to park, we saw the driver—realizing he had failed to block us—skid to a stop.

Then, with wheels spinning, he backed up to the parking lot entrance. He was seeking a personal confrontation!

Quickly we decided to drive through the parking lot, out another exit, and across the street to the police station. The truck didn't follow.

We were justifiably alarmed. In Bridgeport the previous year another driver, angered at being cut off, followed the offending car, and shot and killed the driver.

Most angry drivers don't shoot, threaten to shoot, or even carry a gun. Few actually seek a personal confrontation. But most angry drivers do punish "bad" drivers. Cursing, shouting, horn honking, obscene gestures, scowling faces, and clenched fists are a common sight on our nation's highways.

HOW ANGRY CAN YOU GET?

Driver anger is exacerbated by roads that are crowded with more than double the number of cars of twenty years ago, while road capacity has increased by only 11 percent. Construction projects, rush-hour commuting, large tractor-trailers, accidents, and rubber necking hamper driving and increase frustration.

But the major responsibility for driver anger lies with the driver, not the highway.

While this statement seems like an outrageous proposition to drivers inclined to become angry easily, consider for a moment the example mentioned above. Frank did not hit the truck whose driver became so angry. He made an instinctive move toward the left lane when faced with the stalled car, but he did not try to force the truck to yield, and he stopped in plenty of time to let the truck pass. Understandably, the truck driver would have experienced a momentary feeling of anxiety when he thought about what might have happened if Frank had kept coming.

"Wow, that was a close call," he might (appropriately) have thought to himself afterward.

The truck driver's reaction was significantly stronger. He was enraged by an action that he considered a threat to his safety. He was out for blood. On a scale from zero to ten (see Anger Intensity Scale, below), where zero denotes complete contentment, and ten expresses the highest degree of killing rage of which we are capable, the truck driver's response had to have been at least eight. We feared it might have been ten. It was an overreactive response to a close call, a relatively common but minor occurrence. I say overreactive because it is unlikely that he would have gotten much angrier even if an accident had actually occurred.

Consider: Would the truck driver's anger have been any worse if Frank had actually hit him? Would he have murdered over an accident? Suppose an accident had occurred and the truck driver had broken his leg, and was off work for six weeks. Would he have been any angrier? What if, in addition, his truck had been totaled, and he had lost his job? Angrier still?

Probably not. But asking these questions puts into sharp focus what I mean when I say that the major responsibility for a driver's anger lies with the driver, not the highway. In the encounter with the truck driver, circumstances justified a stress reaction on his part of three to five on the anger intensity scale. This man went up to an eight or more. His overreaction was his responsibility, no one else's.

Anger Intensity Scale

RANK	DESCRIPTION OF MOOD
0	Perfectly relaxed, content, and peaceful
1	Ordinary wakefulness, good mood
2	Energetic, briskly solving problems
3	Trying harder, extra effort, and troubled
4	Annoyance, irritation, and increased alertness
5	Truly aggravated, indignant, and pushing hard
6	Just about had it; combat-ready and going all out
7	Temper flares, adrenaline surges; really mad
8	Furious, ready to fight
9	Rage and wrath, no holds barred
10	Ready to kill, as angry as we can get

You can relate to this scale rather easily, especially if you use that inner anger surge sensation as a guide. When you feel that surge, you know you're at least at a seven. Be honest with yourself—I have administered this test to many, many people, and while you might not like to own up to being one of those who at least thinks of killing, I can assure you that you are not alone. Once you make this admission to yourself, you can feel reassured, knowing that this secret anger doesn't mean that you are one of the "bad people" who actually hurt others.

Over the years, drivers' responses to the question "What makes you angry on the road?" have sorted themselves into five categories. (The anger-intensity ranking indicates the level reached by half the members of any group of thirty or more people over twenty-five years old. Teenagers and young adults reach much higher levels.)

Drivers who put me at high risk:

Truck drivers cutting me off	10
Drivers making inappropriate sudden stops	10
Reckless drivers cutting me off	9
Tailgaters	8
Speeders and weavers	7

Drivers who put me at some risk:

Drivers running red lights	10
Drivers making turns and lane changes without signaling	8
Drivers who signal a left turn and go right	8
Drivers cutting in	7

Incidents that slow me down:

Cars in the left lane that won't yield	10
Unfinished construction	8
Cars not turning right when it's legal	8
Traffic jams	8
Trucks in the far left lane	5

People who intentionally annoy me:

Someone making a face and cursing	10
Drivers using high beams	10
Saturn cars with bright running lights	10
Drivers who suddenly pull out ahead	10
Cyclists and joggers who don't yield	9
Someone giving me the finger	9

People I observe putting others at risk:

Drivers speaking on cellular phones	9
Pedestrians walking in the street	9
Drivers reading newspapers	8
People driving cars in breakdown lane	8
Drivers who double-park with doors open	8
Police neglecting to act; no law enforcement	8
Women putting on makeup while driving	8
Men using electric shavers	7
Drivers speeding in school zones	6
Drivers who are inconsiderate to student drivers	5

Please make your own list of the five things that annoy you the most on the road and rate how angry they make you on a scale of zero to ten. That will help you understand and begin your own process of change.

What Makes You Angry on the Road?	How Angry?
1. _____	_____
2. _____	_____
3. _____	_____
4. _____	_____
5. _____	_____

What is really striking is the high number of people who are very, very angry. In the list of thirty types of incidents, there were eight that pro-

voked at least 20 percent of drivers to have momentary urges that might be expressed as: "I
could kill him. I wish he were dead." Half of these
eight were reactions to being punished by another
driver.

~   Police statistics indicate that drivers are most
likely actually to take action and harm another
driver following highway incidents involving
speeding, tailgating, cutting off, merging, and not
yielding the right-of-way. The Mizell report listed
ten reasons given by drivers who had actually injured or killed someone. Each of these reasons
was given by at least twenty-five different drivers
in highway disputes where their behavior resulted in death or serious injury to another
driver:

1. "He cut me off."

2. "She wouldn't let me pass."

3. "He took my parking space."

4. "Nobody gives me the finger."

5. "They kept tailgating me."

6. "He was playing the radio too loud."

7. "He wouldn't turn off his high beams."

8. "She was driving too slowly."

9. "He kept honking."

10. "He tried to run me off the road."

When we read these, we are shocked by the trivial nature of the reasons given. These don't sound like justification enough to actually harm or kill someone.

Yet they are no different from the reasons given by the 20 percent of aggressive drivers I've interviewed who have thought and felt a momentary urge to kill, but didn't. In other words, ordinary drivers like you and me.

It is easy to imagine how, when fueled by over-reactive anger, trivial highway events can escalate into full-blown rage by one or both drivers involved. Road rage represents the culmination of an escalating sequence of punitive behaviors meted out by one driver to another, as reprisal or vengeance for some perceived wrong. As mentioned in chapter 2, there are four steps:

- First Step: A single gesture, curse, or grimace delivered as retaliation;

- Second Step: Repeated and protracted exchanges of the same by both drivers;

- Third Step: Harassing the other driver by tailgating, edging him over, blocking, etc. (highway madness: driver begins losing good judgment);

- Fourth Step: Intentionally damaging another driver's car, or injuring his or her person (road rage).

If someone cuts in front of you, do you escalate the event into a war, or do you let it go? The highway event—the other driver cutting in—triggers your reaction, but the extent of your reaction is your responsibility. How far will you go to redress the "wrong"? Will you turn from Dr. Jekyll into Mr. Hyde? Compare your reactions to those described in the next chapter.

I met Hank in a video store when I needed help putting together a short video on road rage for a speech in Michigan. In his early thirties, of average height and build, he exuded energy as he smiled courteously and asked how he might help me. I explained that I wanted to reassemble a video—put it together in a different order so it told a coherent story. He spent an entire hour helping me to complete the job on one of the store's pieces of equipment. Though I didn't purchase the item we used, he was kind, helpful, and generous with his time.

I did buy several videotapes, and as we were chatting while I paid him (he refused the tip I offered him for his time), he said to me, "Sometime, I should tell you about some of my own experiences on the road." I invited him to tell me about one right then, and this is what he said:

"I get outrageously angry when I drive. Usually, I'm in a hurry, because I work two jobs, this one and another on the weekend that I have to commute some distance to get to. Especially, I hate it when some bonehead won't pull over to let me pass. Just the other day this guy in a BMW not only wouldn't pull over, but actually slowed down in front of me. I was livid. I shot by him on the right and then cut him off, forcing him to almost veer off the road. Then he got on my tail, and drove so close I couldn't see his headlights. No matter how fast I went, and I had it over ninety, he stayed there. Finally, I'd had it; I reached in the backseat for my shotgun. I'm an avid skeet shooter. I took the shells out, rolled down my window, stuck the shotgun out, and waved it at the guy. He pulled right over and got off at the next exit.

"Afterward I thought What in hell was I doing? I could have been arrested. Yeah, it worked, but he could turn me in."

Were we dealing with a Mr. Hyde? Yes! He must have been steaming, clearly above a seven on the Anger Intensity Scale, to have brandished a shotgun. Was he at a ten? He could have been.

I asked Hank if he would be interested in participating in a seminar that might help him; it would not cost him anything, and would be a way I could repay him for the time he had taken with me. He agreed, and he came to two three-hour sessions I led for him and four other aggressive drivers.

He proved to be a very bright guy, terribly overworked and strung out, who had been going all out trying to make ends meet by working two jobs. He rapidly learned the concepts put forward in this book, and when I last talked to him, had stopped having confrontations like the one he described.

There is something about driving an automobile that puts people in a completely different frame of mind than they would be in when they are walking down the street, meeting in a restaurant, or standing in line at a bank. The kindly, polite Dr. Jekyll you meet in church can be transformed into an aggressive Mr. Hyde while driving his car out of the church parking lot.

I know because it happened to me thirty years ago. It embarrasses me to tell about it now. I am a physician and, I'm sure my patients and colleagues will tell you, a compassionate one. But on the road, I became Mr. Hyde.

On one occasion, late for an 8:00 P.M. curtain at

Jacob's Pillow, a theater in western Massachusetts, I became enraged at a slow-moving Cadillac blocking my way along the winding two-lane highway. Neither the sound of my horn nor the flash of my lights caused the guy to pull over. Finally, on a short strip of open road, I recklessly passed him.

Once by him, I felt an urge to get revenge for the "wrong" done me, and I abruptly applied my brakes, just enough to cause the alarmed Cadillac driver to slam on his. Then, just before impact, I gunned my motor and sped away, exulting over "teaching him a lesson."

Even now, thirty years after my "revenge," and no longer holding the view of driving that I had in those days, I can feel the adrenaline rush when I recall the images and feelings of that night.

Measured on the scale at the end of chapter 5, my vendetta with the Cadillac driver reached the third degree of anger and risky driving; I was beginning to lose good judgment. By passing him I saved one minute in covering the remaining 2 miles. For this I risked making a dangerous pass; I risked a possible collision; and I certainly caused three other people, one in my car and two in his, to have their hearts in their throats. I allowed my "Mr. Hyde" to take over, taking tremendous risks, but at no point intending to damage his car or seek a personal confrontation.

But what about incidents that escalate into physical violence, even one-to-one combat? Can the Jekyll-and-Hyde syndrome explain those, too?

In Roanoke, Virginia, twenty-two-year-old Whitney Hollingsworth was speeding, going 60–70 mph in heavy traffic, hurrying to meet her brother at a shopping mall, when she saw Charles Draper race up behind her and flash his lights, seeking to pass. Whitney refused to pull over. She reasoned she was going fast enough, and the other driver was not going to be able to go much faster even if he passed her, because of the heavy traffic.

Responding to Whitney's intransigence, Charles drove up closer, tailgating her, so close she couldn't see his headlights.

Growing annoyed and anxious, she put on her brakes "to tell him to back off." Charles slammed on his brakes to avoid a collision. He became instantly alarmed and then furious. He did not experience Whitney's behavior as a "request" to back off; instead he perceived it as a threat and a challenge.

He became angrier, and pulled up alongside Whitney on her right. They exchanged scowls, curses, and obscene gestures. Charles followed Whitney, and when she turned at the shopping mall exit, he turned off, too, passing her on the exit ramp.

Then he put on his brakes, and Whitney had to stop. Charles walked back to Whitney's car, asking her to step outside. She refused. He opened her door and pulled her from the car, then spat in her face. She slapped him. He struggled with her, trying to force her into the path of other cars going by on the exit ramp. Finally one driver stopped and said, "Hey, you're blocking traffic."

Charles replied, "She put her brakes on in front of me and I almost ran into her."

The other driver said, "So?"

Whitney said, "So?"

Charles let go of Whitney, shrugged his shoulders, walked back to his vehicle and drove away without another word.

Would this have occurred if Whitney had yielded the right-of-way when Charles first flashed his lights? Of course not. Would this have occurred if Whitney hadn't put on her brakes? No.

Yes, Charles started it by tailgating, driving too close, and harassing Whitney with his high beams. But if Whitney had been interested in preventing violence rather than taking the law into her own hands, "punishing" Charles by suddenly braking while traveling at a high speed, the violence wouldn't have happened.

People like Charles and Whitney play by different rules on the highway than if they met walking down the street. Charles wouldn't walk up behind Whitney and say, "Get out of the way, I want to get by." Whitney wouldn't reply, "No way, I was here first." Charles wouldn't respond by walking up so close to Whitney she could feel him breathing down her neck. Whitney wouldn't reply to that by abruptly stopping, or turning to face Charles, directly challenging him.

Yet people do equivalent things on the road.

Notice how quickly Charles's anger evaporated once he left his car, and was listened to by the passing motorist. That short conversation ended his rage. Why? One moment earlier he was trying to throw Whitney into oncoming traffic. How come he snapped out of it so quickly? The answer is that once the motorist suggested another point of view, Charles calmed down immediately. Charles isn't a malevolent "thrill killer."

Almost all violence on the road begins when one driver feels wronged by some aggressive or risky driving behavior by another driver and decides to retaliate in some manner. The first driver perceives this retaliation as an assault and retaliates in turn, thus escalating the conflict. Once engaged, each driver refuses to stop for fear of losing face. Charles and Whitney were lucky that a neutral person happened by and interrupted their fight to the finish.

Are Charles and Whitney unusual? Not particularly. I have found three groupings of individuals
prone to violence, who are likely to escalate a minor
road incident until it becomes violent:

- Young males, eighteen to twenty-six, poorly
  educated, many with criminal records, with
  past histories of drug and alcohol prob-
  lems, often described by friends and relatives as loners;

- "Hard chargers": successful men and
  women, with no known histories of crime,
  violence, or drug or alcohol abuse, often
  stressed-out from work or personal troubles, who seem to snap;

- Distraught men and women with recent injuries to their self-esteem due to relationship breakup, divorce, job loss, or disabling
  injury, who become easily provoked by
  perceived threats to their remaining self-
  esteem.

All of the hundreds of aggressive, angry drivers I've treated, including those who've been violent, must have been Jekyll-and-Hydes. Certain
qualities of "road ragers" emerge that distinguish
them from other perpetrators of violence:

- They have no criminal history;

- They're not violent off the road;

- They're courteous off the road;

- If they are walked away from their vehicle
  by a police officer, they immediately calm

down, usually becoming contrite and apologetic;

- They often feel like a victim, having acted in self-defense, and after the incident, if not influenced by legal considerations, they will acknowledge that they got out of hand.

How many of us are likely to become annoyed behind the wheel? One-third of a seventy-five-member audience I addressed said they had encountered a hostile driver the previous week. Fifteen people said that they had initiated the exchange. In just one week, roughly 20 percent of the group became Mr. Hydes.

Could that be right? *Twenty* percent?

Over the past five years I've administered the Larson Driver Stress Profile to people in the following groups: teenagers in driver training; stressed individuals seeking treatment at the Larson Institute of Stress Medicine; aggressive drivers recruited by two AAA Connecticut Clubs; driving school instructors; participants in the Coronary/Cancer Prevention Project; patients who have had heart attacks; psychiatric staff members at Norwalk Hospital; drivers with a history of road rage; and college students attending a seminar at the University of Connecticut.

In addition, the Michigan State Police administered a shorter, twenty-question version of the test to 875 adults, ages eighteen and over, chosen randomly from Michigan and from four other parts of the United States.

Looking at the results from all of these groups, we can approximate the percentage of very angry drivers, and can estimate how many could change into Mr. Hydes given provocative highway incidents.

For the twenty-eight drivers, aged twenty-eight to seventy-two, who participated in the Larson Driver Attitude Change Seminar, sponsored by the AAA Foundation for Traffic Safety and by two Connecticut AAA clubs, the Larson Driver Stress Profile results were as follows:

Low	7
Moderate	6
High	15

Tests administered to ten drivers with a history of road rage, who have harassed, harmed, provoked, or endangered other drivers yielded these scores:

Low	0
Moderate	1
High	9

In this small sample, 90 percent of road rage incidents happen to drivers whose Larson Driver Stress score is thirty-five or above. Just how many drivers score in this "high" range?

The New Jersey Insurance News Service sponsored a driver survey to determine the percentage of aggressive drivers on the roads. In June 1998, twenty-five New Jersey AAA club offices administered the Larson Driver Stress Profile to over four hundred New Jersey drivers, asking them to score themselves in the four categories of anger, impatience, competing, and punishing. The results were as follows:

Anger	23.8 percent high, 30.4 percent moderate
Impatience	12.3 percent high, 34.2 percent moderate

| Competing | 10.5 percent high, 75 percent moderate |
| Punishing | 19.5 percent high, 21.5 percent moderate |

Overall, the score was 12 percent high, 30 percent moderate.

The most alarming statistic is that 41 percent of these drivers indicated that they punish other drivers. The overall score indicates that 12 percent of these four hundred-plus drivers, about fifty of them, are highly aggressive. This, together with the "Anger" and "Punishing" scores of roughly 20 percent, reflects the number of highly aggressive drivers on the roads, drivers potentially likely to be involved in a road-rage incident. If you challenge one of them, you are likely to become involved in a road-rage incident, too. Whether or not you choose to challenge a rude, aggressive driver depends on how you derive your self-esteem, and that is the subject of the next chapter.

Oscar Salinas, driving with his friend Joaquin in Houston, Texas, tried to stop, but poor brakes failed and his auto tapped the rear bumper of a pickup truck. No damage was done, and Oscar drove away, but the pickup followed. The driver pulled abreast of the car and someone inside the truck cab shot and killed Oscar, critically wounding Joaquin.

Why shoot? The pickup truck wasn't damaged. Since the driver's property wasn't damaged, what was? Something much more important: his self-esteem. Remember, anger arises when your beliefs are challenged. The shooter could have believed something like, "No one messes with me and gets away with it." If he allowed Oscar to "get away with" tapping his bumper, then he would lose face; this would damage his already flagging self-esteem even further. That could not happen, so he shot. After shooting he could think, "See, I'm the kind of guy no one messes with."

Sound crazy? While this is an extreme example, we all operate by trying to enhance our self-esteem. We all want to feel good about ourselves—proud, content, and self-confident. We don't want to feel bad—ashamed, guilty, and inferior. We will do whatever we believe necessary to produce the former feelings, and avoid doing what results in the latter.

There are two basic ways we go about this: by setting goals and achieving them, and by enjoying personal relationships and the pleasures of simply being alive.

The first way of achieving self-esteem is by setting goals for ourselves, goals related to achievements, tasks, or dreams. When we reach them we feel good; our self-esteem is positive. If we exceed our goals we feel exultant. Just watch the frenzied exuberance of sports team members just after the final victory bringing them the championship: baseball players will jump into a pile, hugging, laughing, shouting, and congratulating each other. On no other occasion do grown men behave this way.

On the other hand, when we fall short of our goals we feel bad; we have negative self-esteem. If we fall way below our expectations, we feel despondent. A team losing the championship game they were favored to win will become clinically depressed; players will cry, hang their heads (often covering them with towels), or stare vacantly into space, averting their eyes. For them it's not just another game.

On the highway we may invest goals with greater importance than they deserve. We may not be aware that we're doing this. When we do we set ourselves up, needlessly, for a self-esteem battle. For example, something as simple as driving time to a destination may become a goal linked to self-esteem if we invest it with too much importance. "Driving time" becomes more than simply driving time. It becomes a personal contest. If we make it within the time we've set, we "win" and we feel good. If we don't, we lose and we feel bad. When we invest too much in meeting such goals, we'll become angry at whatever or whoever has thwarted us. Because we have such a personal self-esteem investment in achieving the goal, we will experience any event or driver that delays us as acting against us, personally, because we've made it into a personal issue. If we do this a lot, we'll become enraged frequently.

•   •   •

Listen to Jill, a no-nonsense, energetic, middle-aged woman who became frustrated when she couldn't meet her driving-time goal:

"I drive to our farm in Vermont every Friday night. From Westport it takes me three hours door to door. When the traffic moves right along I feel fine, although I do find myself getting tense if it begins to rain. I'm afraid we might be delayed. There can be a real traffic tie-up going through Hartford. I really get irritable then. I can't stand to be late, so when that happens I get mad all over again at those imbeciles who designed the Hartford interchanges. Once we get past Springfield I can relax. Although once, I remember, I missed the turnoff at Brattleboro. So stupid! I was furious with myself. Fred, my husband, kept telling me to calm down. Poor man. One time he had some type of stomach upset and had to keep stopping at practically every filling station along the road to use the rest room. I'm afraid I was not very gracious about it and we had a furious row."

Faced with a delay that made it impossible for her to achieve her three-hour goal, Jill felt anxious and apprehensive; these feelings were swiftly followed by irritation and anger. When she blamed her husband and his "inconsiderate" diarrhea she felt hate. And her marriage wasn't the only thing that suffered. The stress hormones generated by all that anger contributed to Jill's hypertension.

There must be another way to achieve self-esteem! The second way we achieve self-esteem is from experiencing in our bodies the warmth from liking or loving and being liked or loved in return. When we experience our affection and love for another we feel good; our self-esteem is positive. When that individual loves us back we feel even better.

I believe the experience of love and affection stems from a relationship where we feel understood and appreciated; it is enhanced by understanding and appreciating the other person. I don't believe love is something we do; we cannot turn love on through willpower. Love is something we experience when we "connect" with another—when we understand and appreciate the other. It is nature's way of inducing us to make connections to others; we get a rush, an emotional reward.

But relationships take time and attention; the better we listen and the better we communicate, the more we feel love. Jill's excessive personal investment in achieving her three-hour travel time made her so preoccupied that she was unable to listen to and understand her husband's anguish. Her ability to share herself with her husband was impaired because her attention was divided. Imagine that Jill had focused on her husband's comfort, rather than her travel time. They could have stopped for an hour and given him time to recuperate. He would have felt loved and appreciated. She could have relaxed and enjoyed a cup of tea and felt the warmth of his love and appreciation. I guarantee that her positive self-esteem in this scenario would far exceed any self-esteem that she could have derived from meeting her travel time.

We can't have it both ways. Our effort to gain self-esteem through reaching our destination on time costs us the self-esteem we could have obtained if we were more engaged with our passengers.

Not only can we reduce our anger, but we can increase our self-esteem and our happiness. It all hinges on whether we get our self-esteem from setting goals and achieving them, or from our relationships. How we get our self-esteem depends on what we believe is important. The good news is that we have the ability to choose our beliefs. All we have to do is identify the beliefs we are currently operating under, understand the new alternative beliefs that would give us self-esteem in more life-enhancing ways, and flip to the new beliefs. It's easier than it sounds.

In *The Power of Myth*, a famous public television documentary, Bill Moyers interviewed Joseph Campbell, the brilliant religious scholar. Campbell made clear that the power of beliefs is awesome. Some people will die to preserve beliefs that others consider silly or trivial. This is so because deeply held beliefs are bound to brain circuitry and going against them triggers major physiological responses. An authoritative medical journal gave the account of a Haitian man, a devout believer in voodoo, who believed that if he ate chicken he would die.

One evening, a friend of his, who thought voodoo was nonsense, secretly served the man chicken, disguised by other meats and vegetables in a stew. A year after the meal, to demonstrate to the Haitian the groundlessness of his fear, the friend told him the truth about the stew's ingredients.

"Now you see how stupid your superstitions are? You didn't die after you ate chicken and it's been over a year," he said triumphantly.

Then, within moments, he watched in horror as the Haitian collapsed and died, a victim of cardiac arrest brought on by an enormous outpouring of adrenaline. This account convincingly demonstrates the powerful influence of beliefs on behavior.

Anger or distress occurs when beliefs are challenged. Many drivers believe in "making good time," with a fervor that approaches the Haitian's. It is a fervor strong enough to justify killing another human being or driving in a self-destructive manner.

People are dying on the highway to preserve

their personal myths. For most road-rage drivers the virtue of making good time determines more driving behavior than "Do unto others as you would have others do unto you." I'm not saying this to claim a moral high ground. It is simply a fact, observed hundreds of times, that the person who would be kind and considerate of your feelings in church might cut you off on the highway in the twinkling of an eye if that was the only way to stay on schedule.

That's because there is no such thing as a stand-alone belief. The brain doesn't operate that way. Beliefs exist within specific contexts. The context the person is operating within determines his or her reaction. The way we talk around the Thanksgiving table is going to be different from the way we talk around a campfire. In one place an off-color joke may invite scorn, whereas in the other the same joke may produce gales of laughter.

Most adults, when playing a game like checkers with a child, will behave differently than when playing the same game with an adult. We may let the child win by letting him take a bad move over, pointing out a good move to him, or avoiding a powerful move ourselves in favor of a weaker one. However, Dr. Meyer Friedman, the eminent cardiologist, observed that many Type A, heart-attack-prone men will play the game with a child with the same intensity they would with an adult. Their context doesn't shift, even though the reality has shifted. These men will defend this rigidity if questioned by saying something like, "He has to learn that the world is a competitive place." Of course, their attitude is more likely to cause the child to decide, "It's useless to try to compete," and the child may stop playing games with such an individual.

On the road, often individuals will imagine

themselves to be in one context, when, in fact, they are in another. Like Walter Mitty, they are living in a world of their own imagination. The Larson Driver Attitude Change Seminar shows people how to shift their context from rigid beliefs about the other driver's behavior and motivation to a more flexible appreciation of why the other driver might be behaving the way he is. At the same time, this shift requires learning new ways of deriving self-esteem—away from achieving rigid goals and toward appreciating life and relationships.

The approach to changing aggressive driving described here is fundamentally different from previous behavioral methods, which tried, through various techniques, to persuade drivers to slow down, wear seat belts, be courteous, signal before changing lanes, obey the rules of the road, etc., etc. This old behavioral approach doesn't work, even though it continues to be where many states still direct their major efforts.

Instead, we regard aggressive driving behaviors as symptoms of the underlying problem. This is a common medical and psychological practice.

For example, if a person goes to his doctor complaining of pain in his chest, easy fatigue, shortness of breath, and rapid heartbeat, the doctor does not prescribe aspirin for pain, sleep for fatigue, exercise for shortness of breath, and sedatives for rapid heart. Instead, she asks herself: "What could account for all these symptoms?" Her answer: "We have a heart problem!"

The same is true for the person coming in to see me for symptoms connected with aggressive driving: impatience, speeding too fast for conditions, irritability, temper explosions, poor judgment, risky driving behavior, inconsiderateness toward his passengers, and lack of compassion for other drivers. I don't conclude, "This person needs to learn the rules of the road and the importance of obeying the laws, and take tranquilizers to calm down." Most of the individuals I treat have a stress disorder. Such disorders come about through excessive secretion of the three stress hormones, adrenaline, noradrenalin, and cortisol. Stress hormones race through the blood of every driver who holds strongly to any of the five stressful driving attitudes, never mind all of them.

Holding to stressful driving attitudes or beliefs, not ignorance of the law, is the cause of aggressive driving. It follows that after the aggressive driver is persuaded to stop driving with these five attitudes, his or her aggressive driving will disappear. This cannot be done by telling the aggressive driver to stop speeding, competing, blocking, scorning, or punishing. The brain doesn't work that way. The brain doesn't stop anything. What the brain does do is start something new. Then the old attitude fades away through disuse. The process applies even in something as natural as falling asleep: we don't stop wakefulness, we begin sleep. We don't stop crawling as babies, we begin walking. We don't stop walking as adults, we begin running.

Does this mean that every aggressive driver will need years of therapy to change his or her attitudes? No! These changes are much easier to make than you might think. In one six-hour seminar we introduce aggressive drivers to five alternative attitudes that they find more appealing than the stressful ones, and convince them to adopt the new attitudes.

Here are the five alternative attitudes you need to learn:

Alternative Attitude #1: "Make Time Good"

This replaces the rigid time-setter's "Make Good Time." If you believe, the way Jill did on her way to Vermont, that you always need to "Make Good Time" and you feel good when you achieve your travel-time goal, and defeated when you don't, then you need to consider changing your attitude to "Make Time Good."

What is most important is to experience the joy of the journey to the maximum. You cannot see the beauty of the scenery, engage fully in a meaningful conversation with companions, feel relaxed, hear music or words, or appreciate the intimacy of others while you are preoccupied with fast driving or keeping to a tight schedule.

When you allow yourself plenty of time to drive comfortably to your destination, all the anger created by the inevitable traffic circumstances that threaten tight schedules simply disappears.

Alternative Attitude #2: "Be a Number One Being"

This replaces the competitive "Be Number One." If you believe that you always need to win competitions on the road and you feel good when you do and defeated when you don't, then you need to learn to become a "number one being."

Self-esteem is most reliably enhanced by being good to yourself, by treating yourself with all the consideration you can muster. Self-esteem generated by winning some competition is of short duration, lasting only until the next competitive situation appears. The feeling of triumph is mixed with anger.

Self-esteem that comes from being good to yourself, while not as heady, lasts much longer (as long as the good treatment continues). Further-more, it serves to make you more resilient when stressful events occur, reducing the amount of anger.

Some of the ways of being good to yourself are: personalizing your vehicle, keeping it clean and well maintained, giving yourself plenty of driving time to enhance the pleasure of travel, having tapes with the type of music you enjoy, being well-supplied with food and drinks for those longer trips, and thinking of driving as worthwhile and pleasurable in itself (in place of viewing it as time wasted until you get to your destination).

Alternative Attitude #3: "Be My Guest"

This replaces the blocker's attitude of "Try and Make Me." If you believe that no one should get by you or cut in front of you and you feel good when you block other drivers and defeated when they get by you, then you need to learn a "Be My Guest" attitude.

Courtesy is the essence of civilized behavior. Giving other drivers the benefit of the doubt about their motives and treating them with the consideration with which you would like to be treated makes for a pleasant atmosphere on the road as well as inside your own vehicle. An attitude of willingness to cooperate or accommodate other drivers' desires is beneficial, as long as you can do so safely, without delaying yourself significantly.

Alternative Attitude #4. "Live and Let Live"

This replaces the scornful "They Shouldn't Allow Them on the Road." If you believe that other drivers are inferior to you and shouldn't be allowed on the road, and if you get angry at what you consider to be their offensive behavior, then you need to learn to live and let live. This is the belief that minding your own business and using your energy and creativity to make your journey interesting and enjoyable for yourself and your passengers is the best way to focus your time. Admit that you have no power to control who travels the same road. There is no entitlement—anyone can be there. Time and energy spent looking for things you don't like serve no purpose; they only pollute your vehicle with hostility.

Most people are reasonable, well-intentioned, and cooperative. Adopt an attitude that assumes this and looks upon departures from the norm much the same as, when walking along a wooded trail, you would view a rock, hole, or puddle in your path, namely, as an inconvenience easily surmounted.

Alternative Attitude #5: "Leave Punishment to the Police"

This replaces the vigilante attitude of "Teach 'em a Lesson." If you believe that it is your duty to punish other drivers who you consider to be putting you at risk, and if you feel good when you teach them a lesson and bad when they get away with it, then you need to learn to leave punishment to the police. It is rarely helpful to other drivers, yourself, or especially your passengers, for you to assume the role of "high executioner." Moreover, it's apt to inflame the situation, putting you and others at risk of bodily harm.

Taking an attitude that most driver mishaps are not motivated by personal intention to harm, threaten, or endanger others, but rather by speed,

miscalculation, forgetfulness, fatigue, and inattention, reduces anger.

Unfortunately, just being intellectually aware of alternative beliefs is not sufficient to accept them, for
the stress-promoting beliefs are nurtured by roots
going back to childhood. Before they can be sup-
planted by new attitudes, some of these roots need
to be hacked away and the new beliefs need to be
nourished with a little friendly attention. The procedure will be painless for you, and indeed can be
interesting and enjoyable. All it requires is for you
to read, carefully, the rest of this book, do some
simple exercises, memorize new beliefs and simple
poems, and practice, practice, practice, and you will
be amazed at how pleasurable driving will become.
     Now meet Mary, who attended a Larson Driver
Attitude Change Seminar and was able to change
her attitude toward her driving.

Mary's husband was worried about Mary's driving,
and she enrolled in the seminar at his insistence.
Twenty-eight years old and very pretty, with dark
curly hair and flashing though soft-looking eyes,
she would never be picked out as possessing the
get-out-of-my-way attitude that frequently characterized her driving.
     "I'm impatient," she said. "I don't want to waste
time, and I'm usually going all out when I drive. I
know what's going to happen to me if I keep it up—
the same thing that happened to my brother, Jim.
He drove the same way. It happened two years ago
when he was twenty-three. Late one night he discovered he had run out of cigarettes. He told his
wife he was going to run down to the store and buy

a pack. With that he jumped in his car and took off for the market about five miles away along a winding country road.

"He was a great guy, but he drove like a madman. On the way to the store he got behind a slow-moving car. The winding road had no straightaways, but he decided to take a chance and pass on one of the short straight stretches of road just before a curve. He floored it, passed the car, but was going too fast on the curve. He lost control, went off the road, and smacked head-on into a tree. He probably died instantly, but it took an hour to cut open the car to get his body out, it had been so badly mangled.

"I've got two kids, and a good husband. I know if I don't get some help the same thing's going to happen to me. My husband knows it too; that's why I'm here."

Mary did very well in the seminar. Later she had this to say:

"Using the Attitude Change Cards was the key. They were excellent because they reversed the way we normally think. The best was changing my mental attitudes. The seminar helped me to see that I wasn't alone. It made a big difference for me to know I wasn't the only one who thinks of killing people. I wish my brother could have had the course. It would have been a shame if something similar had happened to me."

Mary's Driver Stress Profile scores confirmed her attitude change. Prior to the seminar, her overall score was forty-four, in the high range. Three months afterward, on retesting, it was thirty-three, in the moderate range.

After just one day learning new driving attitudes, people can adopt an entirely different, more life-enhancing set of beliefs. How can that happen so quickly and so completely? The answer is revealed in the next chapter in the secret of the Necker cube.

A friend of mine remembered coming to a four-way stop in Westport. After stopping his car he began to cross the intersection only to find his way impeded by another car going through the stop sign to his right. He stopped to let it pass, but before he could get going again another car did the same thing and forced him to stop a third time. He became angry and rolled down his window to yell at the last driver. However, just as he yelled a profanity, he noticed yet another car closely following that one and he suddenly became aware it had its lights on, as had the other cars. To his chagrin, he realized that he had just sworn at a funeral procession.

His rage disappeared immediately. You've probably had similar experiences, and may have felt embarrassed by your misinterpretation of the sensory data. Of course, in incidents of this type, the shift in perception comes from new data supplied by the environment. On the highway, there is rarely new data to facilitate a change in perceptions, so we need to supply the alternative point of view ourselves.

All we need to do is implant new alternative beliefs that our brain can flip to whenever a potentially stressful driving event occurs. Using the Necker cube, shown below, I'm going to demonstrate how the brain works.

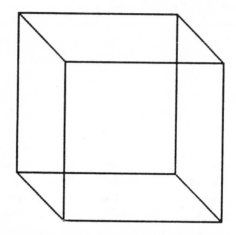

NECKER CUBE

When you stare at it, the cube will appear to shift or flip-flop. First, one of the large squares seems closest to you, and then suddenly, the other one does. No matter how hard you try to keep one of the squares in the forefront, you can't. Moreover, the more you look at it, the faster the switching occurs. And if you make up your mind to view it only one way and then say, "I will not allow myself to look at it any other way," the image will shift before you can finish your sentence.

The reason for the shifting is that the sensory input coming through your eyes to your brain permits two equally valid conclusions. Interestingly, the brain does not see the image as a flat two-dimensional drawing of interconnecting lines (which it really is), but as a three-dimensional cube. Previous data already in the brain convert the lines into a familiar object, a cube. Thus stimulated, the brain fills in the missing third dimension and that's the way the image appears to us. But the brain cannot compute which square is closer. Each is equally possible and our perception keeps switching.

This exercise reveals an operation of the brain beyond "willpower." You actually see two different perceptions, you believe two different "beliefs." You believe whatever your brain concludes at any given moment. Your willpower has nothing to do with it.

On the road, if you can conceive and believe in another, equally probable conclusion, your brain will flip over to that point of view. And, if the alternative conclusion is less stressful, you will automatically become less angry. Even if you flip back and forth as you do with the Necker cube, the time you spend viewing the incident with the less stress-producing conclusion will reduce your overall anger level.

Seeing things from another, more positive, point of view can be difficult on the road. No matter how much we try to find some redeeming quality in the person who has just cut us off, nothing helps; we remain furious. The reason for difficulty in switching our point of view on the road is that, unlike with the Necker cube, we are not aware of all the cues we are reacting to. Indeed, it may not be that being cut off, per se, is what makes us mad; rather, we may believe that in the act of cutting us off the other driver has "bested" us—that's what makes us furious.

From working with hundreds of men and women who tell me of their highway anger, I've concluded that the five beliefs already described are the key elements. Being cut off in itself does not result in rage—annoyance, perhaps, but not rage. Being bested results in rage only for someone who believes he always has to be number one. The good news is that you don't need to come up with a special point of view for each highway incident. You only have to develop alternatives for the five beliefs described in chapter 5 and learn how to apply them, since all stressful highway events are the result of adhering strongly to one or more of the five stressful beliefs.

As in the case of my friend trying to merge into a funeral procession, for any given highway event, you rarely have complete information upon which to base a judgment. Your relationships with drivers of other cars differ from most of your other relationships in that you know very little if anything about the drivers, except the type of car they drive. Most of the time you don't even know what the driver looks like. Your brain has to reach conclusions based on very meager data. Under these circumstances, your conclusions may be wrong; yet, as with the Necker cube, you believe you are right.

If you often get angry on the road and always believe you are justified in your anger, then there is something you can do about it. Do you recognize yourself as holding one or more of the five beliefs? If you do, then you can start by understanding that most of your anger on the highway stems from these beliefs.

The second step to reduce your anger is to fashion new beliefs that will compete for your attention with the old ones exactly at the point when the provoking highway incident occurs.

The third step, changing the old beliefs, will automatically alter the context within which you perceive the provoking incident, and your attitude toward the provoking incident will also change so that you will not react as angrily.

All that's required is that you come to believe in the validity of two points of view. Your brain will automatically switch from one to the other; you can't stop it. Since the aggressive driver is "stuck" in only one point of view, once he sees and believes in the possibilities contained in another point of view, he will begin to switch automatically from one to another. For example: "He's probably not trying to cut me off, he just wasn't paying attention. I've been there."

For most individuals, once the process begins, it does not stop. They will spend more and more time viewing driving from the alternative point of view. Why? Because it is more pleasurable and joyful.

If you are an aggressive driver who frequently loses your temper, and you want to change, I guarantee that you will change if you:

1. Read this book cover to cover;

2. Memorize the five attitudes that lead to anger and the five alternative attitudes that lead to joy, together with the five triggering events;

3. Memorize five simple poems reinforcing the five alternative attitudes discussed in chapters 12 through 21;

4. Recite these poems from memory each day for one week before starting out;

5. Read the appropriate Attitude Change Card (described in the upcoming chapters) each time you get angry on the road, and recite the alternative-attitude poem for one month.

If you do this for one month, after that month you will notice that your anger and aggressive driving occur much less frequently, and those who ride with you will comment on how your driving has im-

proved. As your anger diminishes, don't be surprised if your relationships improve and you feel
better on and off the road. We are almost ready to
take a closer look at the five beliefs and how to
change them. But first, I will teach you a relaxation
exercise that you can use to calm yourself down
either before you get behind the wheel, or when you
want to pull off the road and take a break from
driving.

• 11 CALM YOURSELF WITH THE LARSON DRIVER RELAXATION EXERCISE

How would you like to learn a way to calm yourself down in just a few minutes? The following seven-minute relaxation exercise will teach you how to reduce both your anger on the road and the aggressive driving that often follows because of it. Once you practice the exercise a couple of times, you should be able to enjoy your driving much more.

This exercise consists of three segments. First, there is a regulated breathing segment: breathing in each time to the count of five and out more and more slowly to the counts of five, ten, fifteen, and twenty. Second, there is a progressive muscle relaxation exercise involving the major muscle groups. Third, there is a segment of focusing your attention on the sensation of your breath.

Prior to driving or after you've pulled off the road, just give yourself a few moments to relax. Breathe deeply but without strain, and decide that you're going to leave your troubles outside. Loosen any tight clothing, uncross your arms and legs, and gradually breathe more deeply and rhythmically. As you do this, close your eyes so that you can experience the sensation of your breath.

Slowly take in a deep breath, as deeply as you can, through your nostrils.

Slowly let it out, as far as you can.

Do all of the following breathing exercises slowly and deeply but without strain.

BREATHING SEQUENCE

- Breathe in slowly, counting to five.

- Breathe out slowly, counting to five.

- Breathe in more deeply, counting to five.

- Breathe out more slowly, counting to ten.

- Breathe in more deeply, counting to five.

- Breathe out more slowly, counting to fifteen.

- Breathe in more deeply, counting to five.

- Breathe out even more slowly, counting to
  twenty.

- Take a few deep breaths at your own relaxed pace, then continue to the Muscle Relaxation Sequence.

MUSCLE RELAXATION SEQUENCE

- Breathe in, counting to five and tensing the
  muscles in your feet, calves, thighs, and
  seat.

- Breathe out, relaxing the muscles in your
  feet, calves, thighs, and seat. Visualize the
  muscles and relax them as much as you can.

- Breathe in again, counting to five and tensing the muscles in your back, chest, and
  abdomen.

- Then relax the muscles in your back, chest, and abdomen as much as you can, and let your body become limp.

- Next, breathe in deeply again, counting to five and tensing the muscles in your hands, forearms, upper arms, and shoulders.

- Breathe out, counting to five and relaxing the muscles in your hands, forearms, upper arms, and shoulders. When you've relaxed them as much as you can, relax them even more, and just let your arms hang there like a rag doll's.

- Breathe in again, counting to five and tensing the muscles in your neck, jaw, lips, and tongue.

- When you've relaxed those muscles as much as you can, relax them even more. Just open your jaw wide a couple of times, stretching those muscles.

- Next, breathe out, counting to five and relaxing the muscles in your neck, jaw, lips, and tongue. Just let your jaw hang slack.

- Breathe in, counting to five and tensing the muscles in your cheeks, eyes, forehead, and scalp. Breathe in deeply, squinting your eyes hard.

- Breathe out, counting to five and relaxing the muscles in your cheeks, eyes, forehead, and scalp. Just let your eyes sink back into your head.

- Continue to breathe deeply but without strain as you begin the One-Point-Focus Meditation Sequence.

ONE-POINT-FOCUS MEDITATION SEQUENCE

- Breathe in and out peacefully at about the same rate as when you were counting to five.

- Focus on the sensation of the air entering through your nostrils and leaving from your nostrils. Focus all your attention on that sensation, so you can feel the air as it tickles your nose hairs going in.

- Continue to focus on the sensation of your breath while breathing in and out. If you have any distracting thoughts, just notice them and gently bring your attention back to the sensation of your breath.

- Continue in this manner for as long as you wish.

- At the conclusion, let yourself gradually come back into the car. Open your eyes and look around and maintain the feeling of peacefulness that you've come to.

Practice these three sequences several times in your car before driving, or in any quiet place. They are also helpful whenever you find yourself getting angry at other drivers, feeling tired, or needing a break from driving for any reason. Just pull over at a rest area, close your eyes, and treat yourself to a few peaceful moments.

The relaxation exercise takes about seven minutes. You now have something you can do whenever you get tense, to calm yourself down. If you practice these exercises enough, just closing your eyes and beginning to breathe deeply and rhythmically will get you into an altered state immediately. I guarantee that if you spend a few minutes doing them, you will continue your journey relaxed and refreshed.

The relaxation exercise is used at the Larson Driver Attitude Change Seminar to calm participants down so they can discuss their driving attitudes while they're relaxed.

Now that you're relaxed, it's time to take a closer look at each of the five stressful driver beliefs, and their antidotes.

PART TWO

THE FIVE STRESSFUL DRIVER BELIEFS AND
HOW TO CHANGE THEM

A speeder whose name was Jack Horner
Took pride in his speed round a corner.
He bragged of the feel,
Of his car on two wheels,
Which hastened his meeting a coroner.

Ted, a soft-spoken, gracious, middle-aged director
of a corporation's research and development department, left his home promptly at 7:00 A.M. for a
one-hour commute to his office. Driving as fast as
the traffic would bear, he sought to walk through
the doorway at work just as the reception room
clock turned to 8:00 A.M. On good days he arrived
five minutes early; on bad days he could be five or
ten minutes late. Initially, he regarded it as a game,
something to add interest to a boring ride. However, it gradually became a struggle when unexpected delays occurred. He followed the same
formula going home, thus experiencing this sus-
penseful contest twice daily. This adrenaline-fueled
flight caused a chronic sense of time urgency even
on weekends going grocery shopping. He easily became enraged vying for a parking space. Eventually, I'm sorry to say, Ted had a severe heart attack,
leading to heart failure and a painful death.

A driver who invests his or her self-esteem in
making good time believes and commits to driving
to the destination as fast as the traffic and road conditions will bear. He or she sets either a driving
time, an arrival time, or an average speed that under optimal conditions can be met or bettered only
by concentrating full effort and skill on the enter-
prise.

This sense of time urgency is not the same as being in a hurry. Not all drivers in a hurry have time urgency. The ambulance driver, rushing an accident victim to the hospital, has an appropriate sense of urgency; time is of the essence. However, to have a sense of impending disaster when no real threat exists (like Jill on her way to Vermont) constitutes time urgency—the medical condition. This can become a chronic condition, a persistent anxiety, present even on weekends, and strong enough to prevent you from relaxing on days off.

The driver who merely enjoys driving fast or has to drive fast in a real emergency has no difficulty in slowing down when it is appropriate, stopping along the way, taking time out for lunch or stops for the rest room or the scenery. His or her self-esteem is not invested in the travel time; such a driver simply prefers to drive fast if that can be done safely.

Not so with the driver trying to make good time. Whether it's a trip of 500 miles or 5 miles, a journey cross-country or commuting to the railroad station, driving alone or with spouse and children, this person drives as though his or her life depended on getting there in record time.

Anger results when the rate of speed or time schedule cannot be achieved—and the driver holds someone responsible. Whoever or whatever is deemed responsible for causing the delay becomes the object of rage. A slow driver, a traffic jam, a pedestrian in the crosswalk, road construction, or even a stop sign can infuriate a driver who has to make good time.

How did making good time become close to a national obsession? Here's how it happened to me:

I vividly remember riding with my father the

36 miles from our Wisconsin home to St. Paul, Minnesota. Perched on the edge of my seat, both hands on the dashboard, I felt excitement and fear as he rushed along the narrow, winding, two-lane 1930s highway.

Passing slower vehicles had to be timed to occur on short stretches of straight road before reaching a hill, curve, or approaching car. Father often worked his way up through a long line of cars, passing one at a time and darting back into line before finding the opportunity to pass another. Mindful of daily stories of head-on collisions under such circumstances, I was preoccupied by the question, "Will we make it?"

In those days drivers often passed on hills and curves. They took chances. My father was never that careless, but I can remember numerous close calls when he just managed to get back in line before an approaching car came roaring by.

After every trip, soon after arriving at our destination, my father was always asked, "How long did it take you to drive over?"

"Just under one hour."

I can still hear the response, echoed hundreds of times in the memories of my youth: "You made good time!"

It's easy to see why my father and other members of his generation came to be enormously impressed with speed; they had all traveled by horse. A horse walks at only 4 mph; cars moved at least ten times faster. They had never experienced anything like it.

That meant that the 7-mile journey to town from the farm on which I was born took almost two hours by horse, while a car whizzed over the distance in less than fifteen minutes. Very impressive—that was good time!

As cars went faster, travel times became even

shorter. The value of getting there fast became etched in people's minds, because the wonder and awe of moving so fast had never been experienced before in the world's history. However, making good time has less real value when a speed averaging 40 mph is increased to 60 mph. The additional savings in time when traveling the 7 miles at the higher speed is merely five minutes, scarcely time enough to say hello and renew acquaintance with a friend before the slower car arrives.

I learned from my father. Unlike him, I had no prior experience with the horse; I just adopted his belief in the value of making good time. I took on the value through wanting to be like my dad, listening, and watching his constant articulation of that belief. Consequently, I drove fast, too, and strove to make good time, feeling a burst of pride when I did.

For me, "fast" meant pushing 70 mph, not the 50 mph my father tried for. My son, Chris, now twenty-eight, tells me he had the same apprehension driving with me that I had driving with my father. Once, when he was ten, he wore a football helmet during a drive with me. He was afraid. At the time I did not think his protective headgear was funny, and I reminded him that I was a very good driver. I got to my destination fast, without accidents or speeding tickets.

It really seems strange remembering that at one time, getting there fast and making good time were my top priorities. I did not think it relevant that my son was frightened; rather, I thought that something was wrong with him to be that way. I wasn't frightened and saw no cause to be. Hence, I dismissed pleas from my passengers to slow down.

And I was not alone. Meet Herb, a patient of mine who allowed 242 minutes for his drive from Norwalk to Cape Cod. If he got close to his destination and was running "on time," he would adamantly refuse his passenger's request for any pause in his rush to get there. He would instruct his nine-year-old daughter, pleading for a bathroom stop, to "hold it" until they got to the cottage. His daughter complied, only to develop a serious kidney infection during her teens. Such was the price that *she* inadvertently paid for *his* mania. Of course, he wasn't aware at the time that an infection would be the result; he was blind to that possibility. His desperate quest for self-esteem filled his mind, taking precedence over any inconvenience to her and making him indifferent to her suffering.

Herb suffered from excessive adrenaline as he sped toward the Cape. This aroused state narrowed his focus to the point where his only thought was, "What is absolutely necessary to accomplish my goal?" He unrealistically expected other people to do as he did: "If I can 'hold it,' she can 'hold it.' " And the faster he went, the less he could appreciate conversation, music, food, scenery, or even a desperate plea for help from the backseat.

Herb's relationship with his daughter diminished as his sense of time urgency increased. He thought, "Let's just hurry up and get there and then we can relax."

Yet, paradoxically, time urgency cannot be helped by hurrying. Racing against time actually *creates* the feeling of not having enough time. In order to have the feeling of more time, the driver must slow down. By giving up your dedication to speed, and increasing your dedication to the pleasures of "making time good," you can relax, recharge your neuroreceptors, enjoy your relationships, and, consequently, drive more slowly with less tension.

·   ·   ·

Speed has another downside. The faster you go, the narrower the range of your sensory experience. The faster you go, the less you can actually experience and appreciate conversation, music, food, or scenery.

In physics there is a law called the Heisenberg Uncertainty Principle, which states that you cannot know accurately both the location and the speed of a particle. The better you know the location, the less you know the speed, and vice versa.

The same is true in driving. Call it the Highway Uncertainty Principle: The more you speed, the less you experience where you are. The more you experience where you are, the slower you must go. Speeding, though it gets you to the destination quickly, robs you of the richness of life's experiences. Going very slowly, though it optimizes the richness of sensory experiences, doesn't get you to your destination.

You can only maximize one at a time. Which do you choose? It seems reasonable to choose to drive at a rate that allows you to optimize the journey's enjoyment, but within a reasonable time.

Do you truly enjoy your time behind the wheel? Do you enjoy the full range of your sensory experiences? For example, have you ever considered that there is more than one way of seeing? The quality of our seeing can vary dramatically. There are five levels, listed in order from high-speed/low-experience to low-speed/high-experience:

1. Unconscious seeing: We see, but we're not aware of it. While driving we may miss our exit, or realize we've already

passed a familiar landmark without noticing it. We're not aware of any particular
feeling.

2. Black-and-white seeing: We see, but
we're not aware of color; objects appear in
tones of gray. If we're asked what color
dress someone was wearing, we don't
know. We do have some feeling, chiefly interest and curiosity.

3. Postcard-color seeing: We see in color,
but objects are not fully three-dimensional;
they appear two-dimensional, like a post-
card. We feel pleasure in the beauty.

4. Two-and-one-half-dimensional seeing:
Probably the way we see things when
we're rested and really take time to look.
We see color and some sense of depth. We
feel happy and admire beauty.

5. Three-dimensional seeing: We see in
color, and are keenly aware of the space
between a near object and one farther
away. We feel a supreme sense of awe,
and the thrill of being fully alive. We can't
have this experience very easily without
stopping and taking time to see.

The faster we go, on and off the road, the less
we see. When we speak of improving the quality of
our lives, we would all agree that being able to see
vivid color is better than being limited to black and
white. However, we can't speed without losing that
choice.

The same goes for hearing. Hearing quality
varies enormously along the following dimensions,

listed in order from high-speed/low-experience to low-speed/high-experience:

1. Sound without words: We are dimly aware of a noise, but our concentration on our goal is so great that we cannot distinguish a voice or make out words.

2. Low-impact words: We hear, but the words register faintly, as if from far away. A child may have to tug at our clothes to get our attention; a spouse may complain that we're not listening. We feel annoyed when our preoccupation is interrupted.

3. Clear words: We hear words clearly and react to their content, but the range of our emotional response is blunted by our efforts to concentrate on our goal. To others we appear cold and removed.

4. Musical hearing: We hear the words and the melody and can take pleasure in the sound. We respond emotionally, feel empathy, and reverberate with associations.

5. Sensational hearing: We hear and our whole body is aroused. We experience the sound as a physical sensation. Our spines tingle, our feet want to move, and our hearts and voices want to sing and shout.

To enhance our quality of life, we'd pick musical or sensational hearing rather than sound without words or low-impact words. But you don't have this choice when you're striving to make good time. You only have this choice if you truly want it. Here's how to get it.

Make time good.
Live as though this day's your last.
Learn new facts, no need to fast.
Savor beverage, music, scenery, food.
Companions need time to be wooed,
So take the time to make time goo-o-o-d.

Installation Step 1: Discussion

The first step in changing from a "Make Good Time" attitude to a "Make Time Good" attitude is to discuss how you plan your travel time. Compare your experiences with the experiences of other drivers.

I remember the first occasion on which I decided to drive a long distance at a 50–60 mph speed, rather than my usual 70–75 mph. My wife and I had just spent a weekend in the Catskills, and we started the three-hour drive home. I decided to take my time, enjoy the beautiful fall colors, and share my thoughts with my wife. We had a marvelous trip together. At the slower speed I could concentrate on what she had to say. Since we were not in a rush, we stopped at several interesting spots that we would not have noticed at a faster speed. Moreover, paradoxically, the time flew by, even though the actual travel time was thirty minutes longer. Since that time in 1985, I usually plan my automobile journeys so I can drive at a leisurely rate.

● ● ●

Adding time to your travel plan is the easiest way to begin making time good. Take your usual most-efficient travel time from one place to another and add 50 percent to the time you allow yourself to get there. I do this routinely when I travel from my home in Fairfield County to go to the theater in Manhattan. If the traffic moves briskly, I can park near the theater in about one hour, so I start off at 6:30 P.M. for an 8:00 P.M. curtain. That way I never have to rush and I usually have time to sit reading the playbill in a leisurely way prior to the performance.

Going to church on Sunday morning, where the driving time is twenty minutes, I leave home thirty minutes before the service. That allows me time to sit silently in the beautiful sanctuary for at least five minutes prior to the formal beginning of the service.

My rule is, for drives under two hours, add 50 percent to travel time; for journeys up to three hours, add one-third; for longer trips, add 25 percent, but never drive for more than two hours without stopping to get out of the car, stretch, walk around, or play with the kids.

Sounds great, but isn't it easier said than done? Don't worry, the process of switching from making good time to making time good is not that difficult once you begin to practice. The trick is to get over your resistances to doing it. People who have been speeding to "make good time" for most of their lives universally cite one common difficulty in giving it up. They feel great apprehension and anxiety about arriving early "with nothing to do"! This apprehension is usually masked by the rationalization, "I don't want to waste time."

Take Ted, whose goal was to arrive at the office precisely at 8:00 A.M. He feared arriving early because he couldn't think of anything worthwhile to do with the extra time. This is nothing more than an acute episode of time urgency. Chronic speeding diminishes a person's ability to enjoy simply being alive. The opportunity to have a time to experience the deliciousness of life is thought of as a threat, rather than a gift.

The way to overcome this condition is to plan to have something to do during the extra time. That may be something as simple as reading the playbill or concert notes, eating popcorn or some other snack, going to the rest room, people watching, or telling your companion a joke. In order to adjust to this new state, your brain needs something to do, and will be too anxious to think of it on the spot. Hence, the preparation.

Here I have another rule that is helpful: the rule of three. Agree to try out the new procedure three times. The first time may make you uncomfortable; you'll feel anxious, like a fish out of water. The second time will be better; the discomfort won't last as long. After the third time, you won't want to go back to the old way. You'll know the new way is better.

A second resistance to changing to making time good is the driver's resentment that he or she is the one being asked to change, rather than the slow driver who won't allow passing. "You're trying to tell me it's my fault I get angry and not that dunderhead who won't let me by? Get *him* to change, then I won't be mad anymore."

That would be great, except we have no power to get the other person to change, any more than we can change the course of a river that blocks our way. The angry driver has some justification for annoyance at the inconvenience caused by the person who fails to yield the right-of-way. But the fact that this driver is more than just annoyed, indeed, is enraged, is his or her own responsibility. Giving the incident much greater importance than it deserves makes it a referendum on his or her self-worth, because an inappropriate amount of self-esteem has been invested in reaching the destination within a set time.

As long as the driver thinks that meeting a self-imposed arrival time is a reflection of self-worth, many events will cause rage when they cause loss of time: traffic jams, delays due to construction, bad weather forcing slower speeds, stops to eat or use the toilet, or even passenger stops to look at beautiful scenery.

Try using the rule of three. By your third time, drivers who block you will begin to "disappear" from the highway. You won't be aware of them because they will no longer be that important to you.

Another influence in our culture that fights against making time good is automobile advertisements that extol the virtues of fast acceleration from zero to 60 and of handling ability—the car's capacity to weave and dodge obstacles at high speed. Advertisers clearly understand our fascination with speed on the highway.

In their book *Driving Passion*, Peter Marsh and Peter Collett note how car names encourage aggressive and belligerent highway attitudes: consider "Jaguar—named after a ferocious South American beast of prey, or Mustang—wild and untameable. Cougar, Bronco, Panther, Taurus, Firebird, Thunderbird—all fast and violent animals, real or imaginary."

With so much pulling the other way, it's no wonder we find it difficult to slow down and simply enjoy being alive. However, with practice we can learn to do just that.

•   •   •

Now it's time to learn exactly how to change from "Make Good Time" to "Make Time Good." First, to make your new belief automatic, you must memorize it just the way you would learn a foreign language. If you're studying French, when you see an object that you called "house" in English, you learn to call it *maison*. Then you practice until *maison* is so ingrained that you use it automatically.

Though the process is the same to learn new attitudes for driving, it's a lot less complicated than learning a foreign language. We're not dealing with thousands of words and details, we're dealing with five attitudes. That's why the change process can happen very rapidly: during the six-hour Larson Driver Attitude Change Seminar, or from carefully reading this book and doing the exercises. Besides, the new attitudes are more pleasurable than the old stressful attitudes, so once you begin to experience the pleasures of making time good, you'll be eager to learn more.

Installation Step 2: Attitude Change Card

It's helpful to put the opposing points of view on opposite sides of an index card. On one side write your old beliefs. These beliefs are so much a part of most of us that there's no need to memorize them. However, it's helpful to review them so you know exactly which beliefs you are trying to change in this exercise:

Old Beliefs

Stressor: Setting travel time
Urge: To speed
Statements: Make good time
                 Drive as fast as possible
                 Get out of my way
                 Break a new record
                 Faster is better
                 Stay on schedule

On the other side write your new beliefs. You will be memorizing your new beliefs in the next exercise, so you can choose whether to write them in the form of statements or in the form of the poem that started this chapter. Many people find that it is easier to memorize a poem than a set of statements; however, after reviewing both you should choose the one you prefer to memorize and write it on the New Beliefs side of your card.

> New Beliefs
>
> Event: Setting travel time
> Urge: To allow extra time
> Statements: Make time good
>   You will not pass this way again
>   Savor beverage, music, scenery, food
>   Stimulate your brain—learn by listening to tapes
>   Enjoy your companions
> Poem: Make time good.
>   Live as though this day's your last.
>   Learn new facts, no need to fast.
>   Savor beverage, music, scenery, food.
>   Companions need time to be wooed,
>   So take the time to make time goo-o-o-d.

Installation Step 3: Memorize

To make the new beliefs your own, you must come to know them by heart. The best way is through active memorization. Memorize the "New Beliefs" side of your Attitude Change Card. Memorize both the triggering event, "Whenever I plan my travel time," and the new belief, "I say to myself . . ."

Carry the card with you when you drive; review it before starting out. Once you've identified the old belief and memorized the new belief, the new belief will kick in automatically without conscious effort on your part, just as with the Necker cube. You'll drive in a more leisurely manner, and begin to enjoy your trips more.

Installation Step 4: Debate

Now that you've memorized your new belief about planning your travel time, it's time to use your new language. In place of thinking, "Make good time," think, "Plan or estimate travel time to make time good." Of course, more is involved in the process than knowing a new order for these three words. It's useful to have a make-believe debate between these conflicting points of view. That's one of the exercises in the Larson Attitude Change Seminar. Here's how it might go.

JOHN   (*for "Make Good Time"*). Look, Carol, I like to drive fast and make good time. Time's a-wastin'. Drive as fast as possible, I say. Get there quickly, then you have time to relax. I believe faster is better, and I find it fun to try to break a new record, always lowering the time it takes me. Other cars had better get out of my way; I don't have time to waste.

CAROL   (*for "Make Time Good"*). No way! Your dash deprives you of enjoying your life; you scarcely have time to breathe. I believe I only have one life, and I want to experience it in all its richness; I shall not pass this way again. I prefer to make the journey part of my life, in place of putting my life on hold until I reach my destination. I'm for quality. I want to fully enjoy my companions, and share the sounds, sights, tastes, and smells along the way. Make time good, I say.

At this point change positions: Carol takes "Make Good Time" and John takes "Make Time Good."

CAROL (*for "Make Good Time"*): It's important for me to keep my word and stay on schedule. I want to arrive promptly when I said I would. I don't want to waste time, so I don't want to arrive early. I love the excitement of setting tight schedules and trying to set a new record for the time it takes to travel the distance. I drive as fast as I can, and other cars had better get out of my way. If you don't like the way I drive, that's just too bad. I'm not going to sacrifice making good time to your wimpy attitude.

JOHN (*for "Make Time Good"*): My gosh, you're so blind, you're missing out on life. I want to thoroughly enjoy my journey, and I'll arrive rested not long after you get there. I might even get there first, especially if you wind up wrapped around a tree. I want to enjoy my companion; it's a chance to talk personally without interruptions. We might listen to music or share that tape about music appreciation. I love to sip a cup of coffee and munch on a bagel as I drive. I'd love to share this with you; we might not pass this way again.

Of course, this is not a random, anything-goes debate. One point of view expresses the attitude that underlies gaining self-esteem by setting and reaching goals acquired through effort, stress, and strain, whereas the other point of view expresses the attitude most conducive to gaining self-esteem through self-nurturing experiences.

Installation Step 5: Relaxation Exercise

Reserve fifteen minutes for yourself. Pick a quiet spot, where you won't be disturbed. Elicit the relaxation response described in chapter 11 by taking a few slow, deep breaths, inhaling to the count of five, and exhaling more and more slowly to the counts of five, ten, fifteen, and twenty. Take your Attitude Change Card and proceed as follows:

- Elicit the relaxation response.

- Visualize or imagine planning your travel time.

- Read your list of new beliefs.

- Once again, elicit the relaxation response.

- Visualize or imagine planning your travel time.

- Read your list of new beliefs.

- Try to remember them.

- Elicit the relaxation response one more time.

Installation Step 6: Practice!

With practice, one of the phrases, like "Make time goo-o-o-d," will gradually begin to act like a mantra for you and will trigger the attitude change by itself.

When I was a kid, Burma Shave signs dotted the nation's highways. These small signs, about six to eight in a series, contained a clever jingle. Here is my nomination to kick off a new series of highway jingles:

"Make Good Time" Jingle

Rushing along
Is just fine
If you don't mind
A coffin of pine.
But a gentle passage
Brings a better view
And would be my choice.
How about you?

Make time good.

A competitive soul named Scudder,
To cars, "I'll beat you," he'd mutter,
Till he met a brown cow
Round a curve at his bow,
And came to—right under her udder.

The most competitive driver I've known was Bill, a ruddy-faced, graying Manhattan executive. Bill had none of the characteristics of the road ragers identified in the Mizell report. He was quiet, soft-spoken, polite, even deferential—a very nice guy. He had a lovely, vivacious wife; two gorgeous kids; and a responsible job. But on the road his Mr. Hyde turned his daily commute into New York City into a series of Olympic game events.

Event 1: He rushed through his morning exercises, shower, and breakfast, striving to leave precisely at 7:00 A.M.

Event 2: At 7:00 A.M. he started his engine, so he could clock the time it took him to reach his office.

Event 3: Certain landmarks along the route—tollbooths, the New York State line, the first sight of the Manhattan skyline—served as checkpoints. Did he pass them on time?

Event 4: He'd pick out another high-powered car and race against it to some marker he'd selected, a tollbooth or highway exit.

Event 5: At tollbooths, while waiting in line, he'd pick out another car in an adjoining lane and compete to see who paid the toll first.

Event 6: At coin-operated automatic toll stations

he'd toss his coins in the basket, then quickly accelerate, trying to pass the light before it turned green.

Event 7: During multilane traffic jams, a certain vehicle in the next crowded lane would become his competition. He'd move from lane to lane to keep ahead of that car.

Event 8: He'd arrive, having timed his commute to the minute, striving to break his previous record.

These competitions were fun only if he won easily. If he began to lose, he became angry and intensified his efforts. If the other driver actually joined in the competition, both vehicles would weave to get ahead, and Bill would become outraged if a third vehicle accidentally blocked him from winning. That's when the accident happened. Bill struck a stopped car while diverting his eyes from the road to his opponent. He survived the accident, but went on to have a heart attack because of the stress hormones generated by the relentless aggravation he subjected himself to.

How did Bill become so competitive? I got to know him very well during his psychotherapy. When Bill was growing up, his parents praised him only when he excelled, and punished him harshly for not doing as well as they thought he should. During our sessions, when Bill talked about his father's scorn and demeaning attitude, he visibly shrank into his chair. Eventually Bill incorporated these standards, and inwardly trashed himself when he "lost." When he "won," he felt good. But he lived in a state of chronic tension, never sure how things might turn out.

A driver preoccupied with being number one can convert many common highway events into pri-

vate competitions—another fast car, someone trying to merge, or even a car in another lane during
a traffic jam. He will want to beat them.

For such a driver, anger occurs when the other
driver appears to be winning or actually does win
the contest created in his mind. An impersonal
event becomes personal. But he wouldn't have become angry if he hadn't thought of it as a competition. A passing car would cause no more anger
than a walker who passed him on a trail in the
woods.

Our culture is obsessed with being number one.
On television we watch year-round sporting events,
beginning with the Bowl games in January and continuing through an endless series of contests in basketball, hockey, tennis, baseball, soccer, and
football, each with its championship playoffs. Television broadcasters constantly proclaim "the thrill
of victory and the agony of defeat."

The "vital" importance of being first is stressed
very early in our lives. One morning, during my
daily walk, a young woman riding a bicycle passed
me, followed in a few moments by a man with a
child about three years old seated behind him on his
bike. As the man rode past, I heard him say to his
child, "Let's see if we can beat Mommy."

This cultural preoccupation has elevated "Be Number One" to a guiding moral principle, over both the
Golden Rule and "Honesty is the best policy."

Starting in grade school, then in sports competitions, and later in getting into college, it's easy to
see where the value of being number one begins.
We conducted a Larson Driver Attitude Change
Seminar specifically for high school seniors. Besides their inexperience and mistaken judgment
about what can happen on the road, it's clear that

the unquestioned value they attached to winning highway competitions accounts in part for this demographic group's high accident and fatality rate.

Similarly, Mizell's survey found a high incidence of road rage among young men who had suffered personal losses or episodes of illness, or had had love relationships end or jobs terminated. Under such circumstances self-esteem is very low, and the young men become more prone to trying to regain self-esteem through "winning" highway competitions.

Movies and television teach the excitement of high-speed car chases. Advertising proclaims the advantages of each make of car in winning competitions. A full-page ad in the *New York Times* on August 17, 1997, introduced the 1998 Lincoln Navigator with this bold headline: FIGHT FOR A PARKING SPACE AND WIN.

So what's wrong with competing on the highway? Highway competitions lead to road rage, resulting in violence, accidents, and fatalities. That's because the more you compete, the less compassionate you can be. Modifying competitive behavior in order to show mercy or give aid to an opponent is perceived as self-defeating. Better to take advantage of the opponent's weakness than to let up. Were drivers to remain compassionate, violence would never happen. There's no other way to understand the Jekyll-and-Hyde phenomenon.

Police are quite clear on this. If they walk an irate driver 20 feet away from his or her vehicle, a perceptible change occurs. He or she becomes contrite, apologetic, and compassionate. Just like that.

All of the road ragers I've known are polite, compassionate, and willing to go the extra mile to help out—off the road. They have been taught to compete on the road, and unbeknownst to them, the price they pay is the loss of compassion.

There is one other place where the Dr. Jekyll/ Mr. Hyde transformation occurs—professional sports. As Vince Lombardi said, "Winning isn't everything, but wanting to win is." Men, cordial to each other before entering the arena, willingly inflict pain and possible injury on opponents. Many games, including hockey, basketball, and football, have "enforcers," players chosen because of their size and aggressiveness to find ways of injuring key opposing players.

The sports model best accounts for why certain drivers become competitive when they get in their vehicles. They have been trained to think of driving as a competition. As their competing becomes more intense, their compassion both for other drivers and for their own passengers diminishes.

I told you about my son's efforts to get my compassion, wearing a football helmet to signal his fear. Remember the little girl whose compassionless father refused to stop to allow her to go to the toilet, not to mention Jill's attitude toward her husband's similar need on their race to Vermont.

Competitors don't realize they lack compassion. They all believe that they're compassionate when it's appropriate to be compassionate. Nothing in their education has taught them to be compassionate when engaged in competition.

Eric, a member of our Norwalk seminar, used to refer to stops for gasoline, while traveling with his wife and two boys, as "pit stops." Just as in the Indianapolis 500, everyone had to scurry to make whatever adjustments they had to make so that the competition could continue and Eric wouldn't lose too much ground to the other cars. Some competitors put off stopping for gas as long as possible if they're not far enough ahead of the particular car they're trying to beat. If they stop, the other car will "get ahead."

Following the seminar, Eric gave up competing and his compassion returned. Now when he stops for gas he plays catch or Frisbee with his kids for ten minutes. That way everyone can get rid of built-up frustrations and have some fun. He reported: "I didn't understand why my family didn't like going places with me before. Now I realize how they felt, and now we all enjoy the trip."

One other person suffers from your loss of compassion: yourself. When you really enjoy something you savor it, and savoring takes time. When competition takes over, savoring is lost. You lose part of yourself in order to devote full attention and resources to winning.

Winning what? Beating another car has no real value. Who cares? It's only a game you're playing, and the game has no utilitarian benefit. Is it really worth dying for?

The most serious thing you lose during highway competition is judgment. Making your children suffer reflects poor judgment. Driving in a risky manner to win a competition is poor judgment. Consider the drivers who, seeking to get to the head of the pack, go into the right lane, gain a little on the car in the left lane, and then accelerate and cut in front of the car in the left lane. One day they're not going to make it. Not very good judgment.

Ron, a forty-year-old salesman, shared his story of losing judgment one evening during a highway competition. Hardworking and conscientious, he rises at 5 A.M. to begin his travels selling merchandise throughout New England. Married twenty years, father of two boys ages eight and fifteen, he regrets that his work allows him so little time at home. But he makes supreme efforts to be there even if it means driving 200 miles at the close of the day to attend a school activity.

Ron hustles, often driving over the speed limit to reach his far-flung destinations. He competes vigorously on the road and off, and he drives aggressively, often "taking on" another driver to see who can get to the head of the pack.

One day, on the Merritt Parkway traveling to New Jersey, he got into a race with a guy in a Blazer. They weaved in and out among the other cars, reaching speeds of 90 mph, each furious with the other. As Ron recalls, he had completely forgotten about his wife, his sons, and his other responsibilities; all he wanted to do was beat that "jerk."

It was then that he saw the flashing lights behind him as a Connecticut state trooper bore down on him. Immediately, he realized what a complete fool he was: he could lose his driver's license, and then where would he be?

Ron does not know how to account for it; perhaps it was his utter contrition and despair when he spoke with the trooper, but, somehow, the trooper just gave him a warning. At that moment, Ron recalled seeing the AAA announcement for my seminar, "Controlling Aggressive Driving," and when he got home that evening, thankful for being able to be home with his family, his life, his car, and his driver's license all still intact, he sent in his application.

When he came to the seminar, he really threw himself into it, vigorously participating in each treatment exercise throughout the six hours. And the result? Let Ron tell it: "When I walked out of the seminar that day, I felt completely different than when I walked in. My wife met me. Usually, I drive, but this time I asked her to. I just sat there, thinking. I had a completely different point of view about driving. I have ever since. No longer do I race other cars; it just isn't worth it."

The road is not the place for games.
Better to give yourself royal care.
Treat your companions to the same.
Share beverage, music, scenery, air.
Learn a new way of seeing.
Become a number one being.

Installation Step 1: Discussion

The first step in changing from a "Be Number One" attitude to a "Be a Number One Being" attitude is to discuss how you react to other speeding cars about to pass you. Think about your experiences of being passed by another driver and compare them to the experiences discussed below.

I often share the story of two executives from Fairfield County who came to me with a problem. Workers were arriving in the morning "all stressed out" from rush-hour commuting. They arrived irritable and distracted, and it took some time before they could concentrate on their work. Moreover, the business was losing employees who didn't want the commuting hassles. Could I help them calm down?

Arrangements for a seminar, "How to Drive Without Becoming Hassled," went well, until the executives learned that part of my approach encouraged drivers not to compete while driving. Both men blanched. They feared the workers would lose their desire to compete on the job, as well as on the road. Viewing competition as a muscle that must be constantly exercised, they canceled the seminar.

Making better products to compete for buyers bears no relation to competing on the road. The first is volitional and can be turned on and off. The driver's sense of competition is not volitional, but is an overreactive reflex to gain self-esteem, and he or she cannot simply decide to stop. If it were that easy, people wouldn't risk their lives for nothing.

Making a better product is achieved through teamwork; competing on the road is "Every man for himself." Businesses that run on the latter model, where workers vie with each other, do not produce the same quality or quantity of product as businesses that run on the collaborative model. Experimental research on this dates back to the 1930s.

After World War II, W. Edwards Deming, an American, persuaded the Japanese to use a teamwork, quality-focused model. Japanese carmakers, using this approach, began to dominate certain sectors of the U.S. automobile market.

Making a better product requires concentration, attention to detail, and good judgment. Competing on the road produces irritability, distraction, inability to appreciate subtle differences, and impairment of judgment. I could have helped the corporation to train its workers to arrive at work less stressed, to have a greater ability to concentrate and think and to work together with a stronger sense of affiliation.

The Pentagon had similar fears about diminishing necessary competitiveness when the Friedman Institute proposed teaching stress-reduction techniques to colonels attending the U.S. Army War College. These were the future generals who would lead the nation's forces in time of war. While Pentagon officials recognized the need for stress reduction to prevent increasing numbers of heart attacks among senior officers, they, like the Fair-field County executives, feared that the officers would lose the competitive attitude, leadership abilities, judgment, and aggressiveness necessary to be effective leaders.

Consequently, a rigorous protocol measuring the effect of the research on all attributes of leadership was followed. Colonel Fred Drews was given the assignment of following the officers' progress through the stress reduction program. If he saw any decline in leadership ability the research was to be terminated immediately.

The findings, published in the *American Heart Journal* in January 1985, revealed that in every dimension measured, the officers became better leaders, not worse. Today, fourteen years later, the Friedman protocol for stress reduction continues to be part of the War College curriculum.

On the road, it's much easier to feel good about yourself by treating yourself and your passengers royally than it is to feel good by making up competitions with other vehicles and trying to win them. Competing detracts from enjoying relationships. Moreover, enjoying relationships is reliable and builds affection throughout the journey as the goodwill generated by your treatment of others generates reciprocal acts of kindness toward you. Everyone wins.

On the other hand, beating some other car usually leads to higher tension and lasts only until the next car to compete with appears. The feeling of triumph is mixed with anger, anger that can poison the atmosphere in your car.

Self-esteem that comes from being good to yourself and others, while not as intense, lasts as long as the good treatment continues. Furthermore, it serves to make you more resilient when stressful events occur; they are more likely to roll off your back.

• • •

So how do we make the switch from having to be number one to becoming a number one being? Seeing another speeding car is the triggering event that can make us want to compete. By shifting our attention, at this point, from competing to relishing and improving the quality of our lives, we are practicing "driving ourselves healthy."

Installation Step 2: Attitude Change Cards

It's helpful to put the opposing points of view on opposite sides of an index card. On one side write your old beliefs. These beliefs are so much a part of most of us that there's no need to memorize them. However, it's helpful to review them so you know exactly which beliefs you are trying to change in this exercise:

Old Beliefs

Stressor:	Other Speeding Cars
Urge:	To compete
Statements:	Be number one
	Lead the pack
	Who's going to be first?
	Winning is everything
	May the best person win
	Beat the other guy

On the other side write your new beliefs. You will be memorizing your new beliefs in the next exercise, so you can choose whether to write them in the form of statements, or in the form of the poem that started this chapter. Many people find that it is easier to memorize a poem than a set of statements; however, after reviewing both you should choose the one you prefer to memorize and write it on the New Beliefs side of your card.

New Beliefs

Event:	Other speeding cars
Urge:	To be courteous
Statements:	The road's too dangerous for games
	Treat yourself and your passengers royally
	Be a number one being
	Savor beverage, music, scenery, air
	Exercise your brain, learn new facts
	Enjoy your companions
Poem:	The road is not the place for games.
	Better to give yourself royal care.
	Treat your companions to the same.
	Share beverage, music, scenery, air.
	Learn a new way of seeing.
	Become a number one being.

Installation Step 3: Memorize

To make the new beliefs your own, you must come to know them by heart. The best way is through active memorization. Memorize the "New Beliefs" side of your Attitude Change Card. Memorize both the triggering event, "When I see another speeding car and have the urge to compete," and the new belief, "I say . . ."

   Carry the card with you when you drive; review it before starting out. Once you've identified the old belief and memorized the new belief, the new belief will kick in automatically without conscious effort on your part, just as with the Necker cube.

Installation Step 4: Debate

Next, using the Attitude Change Card as a guide, engage in a debate with a friend, alternating your point of view so that you are articulate and convincing no matter which side you take. Your debate may sound something like this.

CAROL   (*for "Be Number One"*). I always like to be number one. Being first is fun, it feels good. I enjoy winning at everything. That includes on the road. I like to lead the pack and pull out in front of other cars. If there's a big bunch of people following each other, I'll pull out in front of all of them. Good! I don't see how you can argue with that.

JOHN   (*for "Be a Number One Being"*). You can't be serious. Don't you know highways are too dangerous for games? Why would you want to risk your life for some trivial purpose like getting to the front of a line? Look, I say treat yourself royally. You can cater to your self-esteem that way, without any risk. I'd rather turn the time spent in a car into quality time. I can't do that if I'm dashing to get to the head of the pack. I'd rather savor the company, the scenery, and the music—just relax and enjoy myself.

Then switch sides.

JOHN (*for "Be Number One"*). I think the thing is to get there as quickly as possible, beat everybody else, and then enjoy myself. I hate those guys who try to race past me. I'll show them I can be first. I enjoy competing, and if I didn't compete on the road, I wouldn't compete any other place. It's good practice. May the best man win, and believe me, the best man is me.

CAROL (*for "Be a Number One Being"*). John, the road is no place for games. You are burning yourself out. By the time you get to where you're going, you'll be good for nothing. There is a way of feeling good in the car and that is to treat yourself and your companions well. You'll get there almost as quickly and be relaxed—and alive!

Relaxation is not a waste of time; it can be your key to success. Coach Phil Jackson has the Chicago Bulls meditate. Michael Jordan often sits on the bench to rest. Neither activity impairs the competitive ability of the team or the player. On the contrary, they—and you—compete better when rested and not stressed and hassled.

If you still think that competing is fun and driving would be boring without its excitement, remember, no one can simply stop competing without becoming bored. To find a new, deeper sense of excitement, you must also start something new, like listening to some good music or a beautifully written book on tape.

Try personalizing your vehicle with decorative touches that please you; keep it clean and well maintained. Give yourself plenty of travel time; play the radio, tapes, or CDs; be well supplied with food and drinks for those longer trips and take along books and games for the kids. Take time for stops to view scenery, walk around a bit, or play with the kids to help them—and yourself—blow off steam. You're guaranteed to arrive at your destination relaxed and ready to enjoy your next activity.

Installation Step 5: Relaxation Exercise

Reserve fifteen minutes for yourself. Pick a quiet spot, where you won't be disturbed. Elicit the relaxation response described in chapter 11 by taking a few slow, deep breaths, inhaling to the count of five, and exhaling more and more slowly to the counts of five, ten, fifteen, and twenty. Take your Attitude Change Card and proceed as follows:

- Elicit the relaxation response.

- Visualize or imagine seeing a speeding car.

- Read your list of new beliefs.

- Once again, elicit the relaxation response.

- Visualize or imagine seeing another speeding car.

- Read your list of new beliefs.

- Try to remember them.

- Elicit the relaxation response one more time.

Installation Step 6: Practice!

Take the Attitude Change Card on the road with you and rehearse the memorized poem. Whenever you have the urge to compete with another driver, read the card or recite the poem. This will make it easier for you to resist the urge to compete. Do it at least three times. Keep doing it until the new thought is engraved in your memory.

Then you'll notice an interesting phenomenon: there will be fewer cars trying to compete with you. You'll be focused on enjoying your time in your car, not on competing.

Every time you're tempted to compete with another driver, read this jingle, or have a friend read it to you.

"Be Number One" Jingle

Being number one
Can be fun.
Getting the checkered flag
Can be a gag,
But a highway race
Will cause your erase;
The flag you'll earn
Will be on your urn.
So wait your turn.

Be a number one being.

> *Young Michael would never retreat.*
> *No one could pass him on the street.*
> *When challenged by Robin,*
> *Who was even more stubborn—*
> *"I won!" he bragged to St. Pete.*

Automobiles have been around for only one hundred years—just a drop in the bucket of time. We have not yet developed an etiquette of driving behavior. Books have been written about etiquette for other occasions—weddings, formal dinners, dances. One book even detailed the "correct" conversation that a man and woman should engage in if they met on a train. There has been no book of etiquette for car travel. Maybe this book can be the first. Without such instruction, the attitude we take to strangers we meet on the road is confused. Are we in a contest, a battle, or a friendly exchange?

Shocked Los Angeles neighbors described seventeen-year-old Russell Joseph Pirrone as a "happy-go-lucky kid who was very affectionate to his family."

"You can't say enough nice things about him. He was a really good kid. He took newspapers to the church every week."

Russell and a buddy decided to take a break from cleaning an apartment and get a hamburger one Friday evening. In Russell's Volkswagen Beetle, they cut in front of a pickup truck, then stopped at the next light.

Russell's friend recalled what happened next:

"We hung a right. The traffic was still coming. They honked directly behind us, and called us names. Then, they pulled up on the side. They went a little forward, then slowed down. I heard a noise, and looked up and saw the guy with a gun in his hand. We still continued to go forward after Russell was shot, but we started to slow down."

Russell was taken to Pomona Valley hospital, where he was pronounced dead.

Shot dead? For merely cutting someone off! Compare this to driving on the M4, an English six-lane motorway. Most English drivers are courteous and quickly yield the right-of-way to faster vehicles. When a driver sees an approaching car's lights, the slower vehicle moves to the next lane at the first opportunity.

Moreover, the driver seeking to change lanes encounters no opposition from .cars already in the desired lane. Immediately after he flashes his turn indicator, any car traveling there slows to accommodate the move. That's courtesy!

Contrast that with the "Try and Make Me" attitude frequently encountered on American roads. Many U.S. motorists take it as a personal affront when a faster vehicle seeks to pass, especially if the driver seems rude or pushy. Even when the middle lane is open, certain motorists refuse to yield the right of way.

Similar attitudes make lane changes difficult, even when the driver wishing to change lanes signals in a clear and timely manner with appropriate directional lights. As a result, U.S. drivers play "chicken," forcing their way into the next lane simply by beginning the process and making the driver of the car traveling there choose between certain collision or backing off.

"Here I come, ready or not. I'll hit you unless you yield!"

Such behavior results in harrowing close calls, enraged drivers, accidents, injuries, deaths, and even murders.

Of the 187 incidents investigated in the summer of 1987 in Los Angeles where firearms were brandished either to threaten or to fire at other motorists, two-thirds involved circumstances in which cars were passing, merging, or entering the highway. One driver had resisted yielding the right of way, and tempers escalated to murderous proportions.

At my heart-attack prevention group one evening, Roy came in visibly shaken and chagrined. A wiry, curly-headed advertising executive who reminded me of Woody Allen, he was small, intense, and bursting with energy. On weekends he played saxophone with a band that was in great demand at weddings, graduation parties, and other festive occasions. However, unlike Woody Allen, Roy did not have much of a sense of humor.

Roy explained his source of embarrassment: "I lost yesterday. Someone forced me to let him pass. He got the better of me."

While driving in the left lane of Interstate 95, Roy glanced in his mirror, noticing a sports car rapidly approaching. The driver charged up close to Roy, tailgated him, and tried to edge him over. Roy felt challenged by the nudging. He got himself into a contest of wills and refused to yield the right-of-way.

Roy disliked the sports car driver's pushiness and began to hate him. Roy could not bear the thought of "losing" to the other driver; that would be acknowledging the other driver's superiority. Roy became intransigent.

"Try and make me," he said under his breath.

Then, abruptly, the other driver seized an opening, moved into the middle lane, and accelerated alongside Roy. The men exchanged challenging glances. When the other driver gained a half car-length on Roy, he began a game of "chicken" by accelerating even more and edging over into Roy's lane, determined to force himself into the 5 feet between Roy and the car just ahead.

Roy had to choose. Accelerating to close off the gap or even holding his own meant a collision, unless the sports car driver was bluffing. Accelerating would also bring him dangerously close to the car ahead of him. Roy hesitated.

When he hesitated, the sports car moved in determinedly. In another instant the cars would touch, and Roy decided to "give up." He slowed down and let the sports car pass.

As he told his story, Roy's embarrassment, humiliation, and chagrin was palpable to everyone in the room. He believed he had lost. He looked down, refusing to meet anyone's eyes. Roy lost self-esteem and status by giving in and allowing the other driver to have his way. Blockers like Roy get angry when other drivers persist, escalate the competition, or actually succeed in getting in front of them.

Members of the group praised him for the wisdom he had demonstrated in not risking his life so foolishly. Roy argued with us. He believed that if he had "had the guts," *he* would have accelerated and forced the sports car driver to chose between hitting *him* or backing off.

Something very powerful inside Roy brought him to the brink of risking death—he was almost ready to die for his beliefs. It's clear that Roy overreacted to a relatively trivial happening. Of all the causes one might conceivably die for, refusing to be passed on the highway should surely come near the bottom of the list.

Sometimes a blocker's intransigence has caused the death of another. Jack, a participant in a Larson Driver Attitude Change Seminar, told me what happened to his brother, Jim.

Jim, traveling in Colorado on a two-lane road with his two boys, Alex, seven, and Teddy, five, in the backseat, decided to pass a Ford Thunderbird on a long stretch of open road. He began what he considered to be a routine pass. As he came alongside the Thunderbird, it picked up speed. Jim felt surprised and annoyed, but became more determined to pass and accelerated his own car. The Thunderbird responded with equal speed—not enough to pull away, just enough to stay even. Jim, now outraged, swore and increased his resolve not to let the "bastard" win. His children, sensing his excitement, sat up and looked out the window at the Thunderbird and its bearded driver.

Jim could have backed off, but the race took on the aura of an epic conflict between good and evil. The driver of the Thunderbird had no right to do what he was doing. Jim sped faster, now over 80 mph. So the two cars raced neck and neck into the setting sun. The bright light of the sun blinded Jim to any approaching cars, and he didn't even see the blue Mazda he smacked into head on.

Jim is now in prison, serving a long sentence for involuntary manslaughter for the death of the driver of the Mazda. His children, Alex and Teddy, are alive but permanently brain damaged, requiring constant nursing care. The unknown Thunderbird's driver, who successfully put into practice his "Try and Make Me" attitude, presumably lives on somewhere, with his victory, and the knowledge of the three lives he helped destroy and the incarcerated man he defeated.

Jim has had a lot of time to consider the cost of that day's impulse to prevail, an impulse that grabbed hold of his mind, choking off his rationality.

Roy and the Thunderbird's driver regard certain highway events as win-or-lose situations. Once they define the event in those terms, they've put their self-esteem on the line and the situation becomes a contest, a referendum on their self-worth. If they "win" they have a moment of feeling triumphant and superior. But if they "lose," like Roy, they feel simply terrible—depressed, humiliated, ashamed, disgraced.

Many will risk their lives to keep from having that degree of suffering. But some, even in the winning, may feel worse.

What converts such a trivial event into something momentous? If a car approaches from behind at high speed, obviously attempting to pass, why not say, "This guy must be running late. I'll pull over to help him."

The competitive attitude, taught to us a million times while growing up, and reinforced hundreds of times each day, pervades our thinking. Just as other cultures at other times evaluated events in terms of God's will, fate, or moral principles (such as "Do unto others as you would have others do unto you"), our culture stresses "winning," or in the case of blocking behavior, "not losing," or "not letting the other person win."

This attitude "clicks in" without any conscious decision on the part of the driver. Like a Pavlovian dog, conditioned to salivate when a bell rings, we have been primed to view situations in win-or-lose terms; to fight when we think someone is trying to beat us.

I've been both a blocker and the victim of blockers. Early in my life I sought to get around and cut in front of other cars. Then I went through a period when I tried to obstruct other drivers from passing, especially if they were speeding. Now, I have more important things to consider than trying to regulate how fast someone else should drive. My alternative to "Try and Make Me," and viewing other drivers' aggressiveness as a personal challenge, is to treat motorists with the courtesy I would show a visitor in my home. Let "Be My Guest" be your new attitude, too.

"You want to pass me? Be my guest."
"You want to merge? Be my guest."

Assume the person wishing to pass is much like yourself when you've been in a hurry and wanted to pass someone else or make a lane change. Think, "There is probably a good reason she is hurrying, I've been in that situation myself." Make it easy for the other driver to go on his or her way.

Such an attitude creates a pleasant climate in you car, whereas the "Try and Make Me" attitude has a pernicious downside: its negative effect on your relationships with your passengers. Your belligerent attitude poisons the climate inside your car. The focus of attention shifts from a discussion about the play, sporting event, or concert you've just attended to keeping another guy or gal from going on his or her way.

We create emotional climates in our cars as we drive, just as we do in others places where we are apt to encounter strangers. On social occasions when we meet new people, we are courteous and polite to them even though they're strangers. This attitude has developed over thousands of years of human beings living together. It's the best way to begin relationships. It works. We don't even have to think twice. Even if we don't like the person's appearance, we are cordial and polite. But when we are driving, we cannot see the other driver's face or judge his or her sense of humor, intelligence, station in life, or personal attractiveness. All we see is metal, and if we look carefully, the driver's eyes and set of jaw.

Friend or foe? We look for subtle cues in how they drive to make a determination about other drivers' motivation. Sometimes we meet drivers who show us unexpected courtesy: they signal us to go ahead and enter a busy street, stop to let us cross the street if we're pedestrians, or pull over to let us pass or merge before we even come close to them. I've noticed that at such times I feel a burst of gratitude and affection for the driver who shows me such consideration. I am warmed by the gesture and I feel a surge of happiness: "Hey, all's right with the world."

Strange, isn't it, to feel elation over such a simple act. Why? Because increasingly we don't expect it on the road. Politeness, so common in other human encounters, is, sadly, rare on our highways.

If someone wants to go faster than you, why treat him or her as an adversary? You were satisfied with your speed before that other driver came along.

When you intentionally block another driver, you've contributed to the hostile climate on our highways. I have always considered blocking as much of a factor in causing accidents as speeding. Yet blocking is rarely ticketed, as compared to speeding.

•   •   •

You can change your "Try and Make Me" attitude
if you decide to substitute a new attitude every time
you're tempted to block another car. Next, I'll tell
you how to install the alternative attitude, "Be My
Guest."

He's probably just running late,
Desperately trying to keep his date.
And me, I know just how he feels.
I've risked my life for silly deals.
This is not the wild, wild West—
So I'll clear his path, say, "Be my guest."

Installation Step 1: Discussion

The first step in changing from a "Try and Make Me" attitude to a "Be My Guest" attitude is to consider and discuss your reaction to cars trying to cut in front of you. Compare your reaction to the reactions outlined below.

My friend Harold, a highway competitor, doesn't allow cars to get in front of him. And he especially dislikes waiting in lines. For example, when he approaches a long line at a tollbooth, he will drive down the breakdown lane. When he gets to the head of the line he will aggressively insinuate his car between two of the lead vehicles. Usually he completes the whole process very quickly, before the lead cars can close ranks, barring his entrance.

When the shoe is on the other foot and he is already in the line, if another competitor tries to do the same thing, Harold won't let him in. You might think that having been in a similar position, and remembering some courteous person who let him in the line without a struggle, he would be glad to return the favor. Not so. Harold not only likes to win; he abhors "losing," and that's the way he looks at the situation.

When competing, it isn't enough to have a good offense; you have to have a good defense, too, to prevent your opponent from scoring. This explains the lack of compassion frequently seen in aggressive drivers. They don't regard other drivers as human beings struggling like themselves to get someplace on time; they're rivals, members of the opposing team, and drivers like Harold take on a "Try and Make Me" attitude.

Peter is an example of someone who quickly "put up his dukes" when other drivers tried to cut in front of him. When I knew Peter, at sixty-five, ready to retire after a successful business career, a forty-five-year marriage, and putting four children through college and into interesting careers, he continued to lament the fact that with all his life experience he continued to make "mistakes." He had unrelenting standards for himself, and—when it came to merging—for other drivers as well.

He did not have trouble with cars merging from an entrance ramp or where two roads came together to form one. In those situations, he took turns with other vehicles.

However, on a multilane expressway, when drivers were warned that a lane was closed for construction about a mile ahead, Peter's blocking attitude came out. Seeing the warning, Peter immediately moved to the right lane, only to watch in fury as car after car passed him, traveling in the left lane. Those other drivers stayed in the left lane until the last 50 yards or so before the narrowing, knowing that traffic moved faster there than in the right lane.

Peter became outraged. If he had his way, everyone would have moved to the right lane at the warning sign. He tried to enforce his belief that they should do this by driving practically bumper to bumper with the car immediately in front of him, refusing to allow anyone from the left lane to cut in after the warning sign. He had angry confrontations with aggressive drivers, especially right at the narrowing, where cars merging from the two lanes took turns. Not Peter! He battled with drivers who tried to merge. The highest stress reaction in his life came when another car successfully "bested" him.

Peter's fury knew no bounds. But part of his anger was directed at himself for letting it happen. He replayed the incident over and over again in his mind, berating both himself and the "transgressor" in the other car. He had allowed too big a gap between himself and the car in front; he hadn't accelerated fast enough; he had been distracted by his wife's talk. Peter could always point to a "mistake" he had made that permitted the other car to cut him off.

To understand Peter, you have to know about his controlling father. Peter was brought up to obey the family's rules. There was only one right way to do things. He had to shoulder his responsibilities, excel academically, and, above all, not make mistakes! When he did, his father blasted him verbally and gave him a look of withering scorn.

With help from the group, Peter came to realize that his father was not always right. He had made mistakes, too. This new understanding helped Peter become more forgiving of himself and consequently of others. It also helped him to realize that, depending upon which belief he gave priority to, whenever he made choices, he couldn't help making mistakes.

·   ·   ·

For the driver with a "Try and Make Me" attitude, traveling by road is not simply a trip; it's a contest of wills.

I went through a period when I tried to obstruct speeders from passing. It followed my giving up speeding. Though I no longer tried to compete to win, I sure didn't want to lose! Hence, I tried to block speeders trying to pass.

It took me some time to realize the contest existed only in my head. Most likely, there was some good reason the driver hurried. Possibly the speeder was simply running late. He certainly was not competing with John Larson—he didn't know me personally. It wasn't personal; only I made it so.

Also, whenever I blocked someone the drive turned ugly. Everyone involved became angry and the fun stopped. The ugly mood I had created permeated the air in my car for fifteen minutes or more. If I yielded the right-of-way, initially I felt like I had given in, but that mood lasted for only two minutes, tops. I could then turn my attention to more enjoyable things.

I resolved to treat other motorists with the same courtesy I would show them in my home or walking down the street, and "Be My Guest" became my new attitude.

When a rude driver tries to pass you or cut in front of you, assume the person is much like yourself when you've been in a hurry or running late. Make it easy for him. Take charge, roll out the red carpet.

If the speeder is very pushy, tailgating you closely, put on your right rear directional signal. That tells her you got her message and will comply when you can do it safely. Until you do that, she won't know your intention, and may continue to tailgate.

•   •   •

The first few times you practice letting someone get in front of you, you may feel uncomfortable and a little frustrated after pulling over. New thoughts might occur to you, such as, "I'm being a wimp." Or you may worry that "giving in," as Roy looked at it, will lead to your becoming a spineless patsy in other areas of your life.

If you think this way it probably means you are still investing your simple act of courtesy with the emotions of your former attitude.

Remind yourself of your new attitude by repeating the new beliefs to yourself. As you repeat them, you will notice that your frustration will abate. Every time you feel uncertain about your new decision, repeat them again. Within a month, courtesy will come easily to you.

When you stop using energy wastefully on the highway you will find you have more energy for assertiveness where it counts.

Installation Step 2: Attitude Change Card

Changing your attitude needs to be practiced and the new attitude incorporated into your memory. It's helpful to put the opposing points of view on opposite sides of an index card. On one side write your old beliefs. These beliefs are so much a part of most of us that there's no need to memorize them. However, it's helpful to review them so you know exactly which beliefs you are trying to change in this exercise:

Old Beliefs

Stressor:	Car trying to pass or merge
Urge:	To block them
Statements:	Try and make me
	He won't push me around
	She's an idiot/imbecile/jerk
	Lose this round and you're a
	wimp

On the other side write your new beliefs. You will be memorizing your new beliefs in the next exercise, so you can choose whether to write them in the form of statements or in the form of the poem that started this chapter. Many people find that it is easier to memorize a poem than a set of statements; however, after reviewing both you should choose the one you prefer to memorize and write it on the New Beliefs side of your card.

New Beliefs

Stressor:	Car trying to pass or merge
Uge:	Help them out
Statements:	They're probably running late
	Their desperation is not personal
	I've been in their shoes
	Make it easy for them, let them in
	Be my guest
Poem:	He's probably just running late,
	Desperately trying to keep his date.
	And me, I know just how he feels.
	I've risked my life for silly deals.
	This is not the wild, wild West—
	So I'll clear his path, say, "Be my guest."

Installation Step 3: Memorize

To make the new belief your own, you must come to know it by heart. The best way is through active memorization. Memorize the "New Beliefs" side of your Attitude Change Card. Memorize both the triggering event, "When another car tries to pass or cut in," and the new belief, "I just say . . ."

Carry the card with you when you drive; review it before starting out. Once you've identified the old belief and memorized the new belief, the new belief will kick in automatically without conscious effort on your part.

Installation Step 4: Debate

Using the Attitude Change Card to guide you, debate a friend, taking turns on the belief you advocate. Continue until you can be equally convincing on either side. It might go like this:

CAROL   (*for "Try and Make Me"*). I'm not going to let somebody just go around me if I'm in a hurry. I'm driving the speed limit. Why should I let him pass? It doesn't make sense. They're usually so pushy I can't even see their headlights. I hate people like that. They can just wait. I won't give in; I'm not a wimp. If they want to make something of it, I sure won't move over and let somebody show me up.

JOHN   (*for "Be My Guest"*). Carol, sometimes your stupidity amazes me. Those drivers aren't bad people, they're just in a hurry. They're running late. They're hurrying to be on time. It's happened to me, and I know it's happened to you. I've been in their shoes. I say, make it easy for them. Don't make it personal. It'll be painless if you get it over with quickly, just as you would if they were guests in your home. Just say, "Be my guest," let them go on their way, and return to enjoying your life.

Then change sides.

JOHN   (*for "Try and Make Me"*). It really makes me mad when some tailgater rides my bumper trying to push me out of the way, or some jerk tries to cut in front of me. I say, "Block 'em!" They won't get by me. No one pushes me around.

CAROL   (*for "Be My Guest"*). So what if someone wants to get around you? They probably have a good reason. Even if they don't, why does it matter to you anyway? I'm sure you've been in their shoes at one point or another. Is it worth risking your car or even your life? Just say, "Be my guest." Then you can relax and go about your business. You can even have a good time.

Installation Step 5: Relaxation Exercise

Reserve fifteen minutes for yourself. Pick a quiet spot, where you won't be disturbed. Elicit the relaxation response described in chapter 11 by taking a few slow, deep breaths, inhaling to the count of five, and exhaling to the counts of five, ten, fifteen, and twenty. Take your Attitude Change Card, and proceed as follows:

- Elicit the relaxation response.

- Visualize or imagine another car trying to pass or cut in front of you.

- Read your list of new beliefs.

- Once again, elicit the relaxation response.

- Visualize or imagine another car trying to pass or cut in front of you.

- Read your list of new beliefs.

- Try to remember them.

- Elicit the relaxation response one more time.

Installation Step 6: Practice

Take the Attitude Change Card on the road with you, and rehearse the memorized poem. Whenever someone wants to pass or cut in, read the card or recite the poem. This will make it easier for you to pull over to let someone pass. Do it at least three times. Keep doing it until you have memorized the new thought.

Then, you'll notice an interesting phenomenon: you will notice fewer cars trying to pass you and cut in. Your "Be My Guest" attitude allows you to accept the inevitable stream of cars cutting in front of you more graciously, so you hardly notice them.

Every time you block a car that tries to pass or cut in, read this jingle, or have a friend read it to you.

"Try and Make Me" Jingle

"I have the right of way," says he.
"I have the right of way," says she.
"I won't give in," says he.
"I won't give in," says she.

"What fools these mortals be.
Rest in peace," say we.

Be my guest.

The driver of that car ahead
Must be stupid, because her car's red
While mine is, in hue,
A delicate blue.
So I think she'd be better off dead.

Al, a traveling salesman, constantly found fault
with other drivers. This scornful tendency was especially severe after he watched professional football on television. Al had two television sets, which
enabled him to watch two games at once. The longer
he watched, the more irate he became, especially if
both his favored teams lost. He seethed at mistakes
made by coaches, referees, and players. Following
the games, he became enraged on the road at all the
"numbskulls" he would "bench" if he had the
power. Since he did not, he had to confine himself
to a stream of obscenities and graphic finger, hand,
and arm gestures. Finally, his wife had enough and
refused to ride with him. She insisted that he take
a stress-treatment seminar before she would even
consider getting back in his car.

Al joined the group because his wife insisted
and because, not surprisingly, he had had a heart
attack. An incidental symptom Al complained about
was a twenty-five-year history of insomnia; he had
trouble getting to sleep, and would typically toss
and turn for hours before he dropped off.

Al learned the relaxation technique described
in chapter 11, and amazingly, cured his insomnia
immediately. It turned out that Al usually watched
sports programs like *Monday Night Football*, as
well as the late news, so that by the time he went

to bed his mind was reeling with vituperation at a world brimming with jerks. The relaxation technique quieted all that down, and Al began to sleep soundly. A similar thing occurred with his two football games. Though he didn't give them up, following the games he did spend twenty minutes eliciting the relaxation response before driving. That reduced his anger intensity enough to make him reasonably civil on the road. His wife resumed traveling with him after games.

The scornful driver believes that any driver, make of car, driving behavior, or highway activity that fails to measure up to his or her own self-created standard should be banned from the road. When driving with a passenger, such drivers will continually point out the "boneheads" on the road. As the joke goes, anyone driving faster than themselves is a maniac, and anyone driving slower is a moron.

All people who drive long enough will witness careless driving behavior or see a driver they don't like the looks of. Most of us don't react with rage or wish to banish the offending driver from the road. But for the scornful driver, careless drivers provoke a profound sense of personal injury and affront.

All species have pecking orders, and males in particular have an interest in establishing their dominance over other males. Hence, human males are apt to display signs of their dominance through the make of car, the size of car, horsepower, speed, and prowess in driving. Drivers deemed superior are envied and respected; those deemed inferior are labeled and their inferiority proclaimed. Calling someone by an obscene name or making an obscene gesture is like the lion's roar, establishing your dominance and letting the inferior know his place.

We each have ways of identifying ourselves; friends are similar to us, foes are inferior. Even organizations—be they countries, sports teams, schools, tribes, armies, or families—have clothing, symbols, or colors that identify them. On the road we look for signs that other drivers are like us. I immediately feel friendlier to Volvo drivers, particularly those with green Volvos (guess what make and color of car I drive?), and I'm especially leery of pickup trucks, for example.

Caution is one thing. It is a normal brain mechanism, and one that helps us to stay out of trouble. But rage is quite another thing, and rage does not often serve any useful purpose. After all, tolerance of differences is a necessary part of maturation, as well as being the foundation of our country and a source of personal enrichment. We cannot learn and grow except by absorbing and incorporating different points of view at variance with our accustomed ones.

But the driver imbued with a scornful attitude is intolerant of differences and becomes angry whenever he observes an "infraction" of his standard. Common elements that may conflict with his arbitrary standards include speed, gender of driver, make of car, age of driver, automobile decorations, attitude of driver, and the way a driver drives.

Scornful drivers usually have pet peeves that really infuriate them. A telltale phrase indicating you are listening to a pet peeve is the declaration, "They shouldn't allow them on the road!" This expression describes their rage. They want to blot out forever the stimulus arousing their rage. They just want the other driver to go away!

•   •   •

Even when traveling the same road, "scorners" will consistently report seeing quite different infractions. Jay and Peter, two members of a highway stress reduction group, frequently compare notes.

When not bristling with rage, Jay has a bumptious quality. A young Santa Claus in spirit, he can delight children at Christmas when he dons a beard and passes out gifts. Peter, whom you met earlier, is about twenty-five years Jay's senior, and ready to retire after a successful business career. He laments the fact that despite all his life experience, he still makes "mistakes."

Jay can't abide slow drivers in the left lane of his local interstate who refuse to pull over to let him pass. Peter, traveling the same road at approximately the same speed as Jay, seldom notices such incidents, but becomes livid recounting the number of drivers who cut him off. Jay, on the other hand, regards these happenings as routine, just part of the highway scene.

The scorner invariably sees an example of his own pet peeve each time he drives. Jay can't get over the constant thoughtless, obstructionist driving he encounters every time he wants to get someplace in a hurry.

Some common peeves of scornful drivers are:

- Absentminded or inconsiderate drivers who almost cause accidents;

- Drivers who refuse to yield the right-of-way;

- Drivers who stop inappropriately and hold up traffic while trying to make up their minds;

- Reckless drivers who weave in and out from lane to lane;

- Highway construction that blocks lanes and causes jams.

No matter what the situation, scornful drivers "know" the personality and motivations of the offending driver. Without benefit of introduction, they are absolutely certain about the kind of individual the perpetrator must be.

George, a business executive, ruthlessly pushes both himself and those who report to him. George's pet peeve is drivers who seem bewildered or indecisive. They may slow down to make a turn or to identify a street name or building address, or they may hesitate to commit themselves, temporarily holding up traffic. George feels no compassion for such "inadequacy." They are all "fools who shouldn't be allowed on the road." If Albert Einstein had lost his way and slowed, uncertain of his location, George would have been convinced he was dealing with an imbecile.

Even though the scornful driver will grant that such events also affect other drivers, this does not lessen his or her sense of personal injury. "It doesn't matter if it also happened to you," this driver seems to say. "Why is it happening to me?" Jay worked hard, saved diligently, and prided himself on the care he showed his mother and on his generosity to children at Christmas. Therefore, he believed he had earned the right to unobstructed travel. Since he took care of others, he believed he was entitled to the same considerate treatment.

Since it is abhorrent to scornful drivers to admit they do the thing they condemn in others, Jay believes he never blocks passing cars, Peter believes he never cuts in, and George believes he never hesitates. Of course they do, but they have no awareness of doing it; they lack compassion and the ability to view their behavior through another person's eyes. The particular behavior that riles the scornful driver is the same behavior he was scorned for as a child. Jay could not dally, Peter could not break the rules, and George could not show signs of weakness. The punishment by their parents for transgressing was severe. Consequently, when the scornful driver sees the prohibited behavior, it stirs up old pain and rage, which is vented on the perpetrator.

So, how can you change such a long-standing attitude? The answer, once again, is to memorize a new attitude to replace the old one.

That driver looks weird and strange,
A visitor from a distant range.
But diversity makes life fun.
Relationships count most for anyone.
Save energy to create, play, and give.
So say to him, "Live and let live."

Installation Step 1: Discussion

The first step to changing a "They Shouldn't Be Allowed" attitude to a "Live and Let Live" attitude is to discuss our reactions to other drivers we simply don't like. Compare your reactions to the reactions outlined below.

Dan told the group this story about himself. On the way to the train station for his morning commute into New York, he usually dropped his six-year-old son, Ronny, off at his school. Always in a hurry and "running late," Dan bristled at every slow driver, pointing out to Ronny this or that "bonehead" who hindered their progress.

Once Ronny was dropped off at school, Dan continued his rush to the station. Maria, Dan's wife, picked Ronny up at 3:00 P.M. for the ride home.

About three months after this routine began, little Ronny said to his exasperated father, "Gee, Dad, you ought to pick me up in the afternoon when Mom does; all the boneheads have gone home by then."

• • •

Whenever we find ourselves thinking, "They shouldn't be allowed," we can add our name to the list of scorners. The alternative belief is "Live and let live." Welcome diversity.

Next, minimize the event. Pay less attention to it. Don't take it in. Just remember that difficult, challenging things happen to all of us. Dwelling on the event exaggerates its importance. Better to play it down.

Regard the event as just another happening in nature. While hiking you might encounter an unexpected swamp. You wouldn't say, "They shouldn't allow swamps here!" Why? Because you accept swamps as a fact of life.

My suggestion is to take the same attitude toward highway travel. Just as there are swamps, boulders, streams, cliffs, brush, and wild animals in nature, so are there obstacles on highways which are part of the world we live in. Any or all of the following are natural events on the highway:

- Fast-moving, packed three-lane interstates;

- Traffic jams caused by rush hour traffic, construction, or accidents;

- Slow drivers;

- Drivers blocking your lane change;

- Tollbooth lines;

- Drivers cutting in front of you;

- Tailgaters;

- Malfunctioning traffic lights;

- Large trucks crowding your lane;

- People angry with your driving.

That's our highway world. Regarding such events in the same dispassionate way you regard nature will reduce your anger. If you're going to be part of the highway stream, it's better to go with the flow, expecting boulders and bumblers.

Installation Step 2: Attitude Change Cards

Changing your attitude needs to be practiced, and the new attitude memorized. On one side write your old beliefs. As in the previous Installation chapters, there's no need to memorize your old beliefs, since they are so much a part of you already. However, it is helpful to review them so you know exactly which beliefs you are trying to change in this exercise:

	Old Beliefs
Stressor:	Another driver's faults
Urge:	To lash out
Statements:	They shouldn't allow jerks on the road
	There's no excuse
	She's a menace, stupid, and inconsiderate
	He's doing it on purpose
	She's wrong, I'm right

On the other side of the card write your new beliefs. You will be memorizing your new beliefs in the next exercise, so you can choose whether to write them in the form of statements or in the form of the poem that started this chapter. Many people find that it is easier to memorize a poem than a set of statements; however, after reviewing both you should choose the one you prefer to memorize and write it on the New Beliefs side of your card.

	New Beliefs
Stressor:	Another driver's faults
Urge:	To welcome diversity
Statements:	Be understanding
	Live and let live
	She probably has a good reason
	It's no big deal
	I'll use my energy elsewhere
Poem:	That driver looks quite weird and strange,
	A visitor from a distant range.
	But diversity makes life fun.
	Relationships count most for anyone.
	Save energy to create, play, and give.
	So say to him, "Live and let live."

Installation Step 3: Memorize

To make the new belief your own, so you can use it when you need it, you must come to know it by heart. The best way is through active memorization.

Memorize the "New Beliefs" side of your Attitude Change Card. Memorize both the triggering event, "When I see a driver I dislike," and the new belief, "I say to myself . . ."

Carry the card with you when you drive. Review it before starting out, and whenever you encounter the triggering cue of another driver you dislike. Once you've identified the old belief and memorized the new belief, the new belief will kick in automatically without conscious effort on your part.

Installation Step 4: Debate   .

Using the Attitude Change Card to guide you, debate a friend, taking turns on the belief you advocate. Continue until you can be equally convincing on either side. It might go like this:

CAROL (*for "They Shouldn't Be Allowed"*). There are so many idiots on the road, it is absolutely unbelievable! Usually, they are driving too slowly, and swinging way out of their lane to make a turn. There's no excuse for that kind of behavior. I am a good driver and I'd never drive that way. They shouldn't be allowed on the road.

JOHN (*for "Live and Let Live"*). Look at how you're using your energy, ranting and raving about what other drivers are doing on the road.

There's probably a good reason for what they're doing. Everyone has their peculiarities, even you and sometimes even me. Welcome diversity, it's what America is based on. Let people be the way they are. Use your energy elsewhere. Say "Live and let live," and then you can go ahead and live.

Then change sides.

JOHN (*for "They Shouldn't Be Allowed"*). You won't believe this, Carol—do you know the number of jerks I counted just coming here from home? I only live ten minutes away! Six jerks in less than two miles! There was someone who didn't know where he was going. I don't know how he ever got a license. If I had anything to do with it, he sure wouldn't keep it. They shouldn't be allowed on the road if they're going to drive that way.

CAROL (*for "Live and Let Live"*). Relax and stop looking at what everyone else is doing. Sure, people won't always do what you want them to do. Everyone's different. Diversity makes life fun. What counts most is relationships. Focus your energy on enjoying your time in the car and having fun with your passengers. How much fun can it be just counting how many jerks there are out there? Say "Live and let live" and get on with your life.

Installation Step 5: Relaxation Exercise

Reserve fifteen minutes for yourself. Pick a quiet spot, where you won't be disturbed. Elicit the relaxation response described in chapter 11 by taking a few slow, deep breaths, inhaling to the count of five, and exhaling more and more slowly to the counts of five, ten, and fifteen, and twenty. Take your Attitude Change Card, and proceed as follows:

- Elicit the relaxation response.

- Visualize or imagine a driver you dislike.

- Read your list of new beliefs.

- Once again, elicit the relaxation response.

- Visualize or imagine a another driver you dislike.

- Read your list of new beliefs.

- Try to remember them. .

- Elicit the relaxation response one more time.

Installation Step 6: Practice!

Every time you encounter another driver you dislike, read your alternative belief and recite the poem. Then, read this jingle, or have a friend read it to you.

Scornful Driver's Jingle

Counting the wrongs
Of the way they drive—
Blood pressure and gas
Will boil inside.
Look for the right,
Let the wrongs be;
The rights will grow
Most pleasantly.

Live and let live.

> *There once was a young vigilante.*
> *On slow cars he maxed out his ante.*
> *He'd ram them "to scare,"*
> *But, thrown in the air,*
> *He rained down upon Ypsilanti.*

I was a highway "vigilante" once. Not the kind who chased offending drivers for a personal confrontation, but the kind who believed it was my duty to teach "bad" drivers a lesson by punishing them.

For slow drivers who blocked me from passing, I had a variety of vengeful strategies. When flashing my lights or honking my horn failed to motivate a driver, I fell back from the slow vehicle a bit and then accelerated as though I intended to ram him, stopping just short of his rear bumper. I cannot actually remember doing this, but my son tells me he can recall such occasions when he was about eight years old. (Remember the football helmet he wore for safety?)

At night I rode the slow driver's bumper with my high beams on. I often passed the slow vehicles on the right, pulled in front of them, then abruptly slowed down, forcing them to brake sharply to avoid a collision. A variation of this was to slow down to 30 mph, or until I became the slow drivers' "slow driver." When they had had enough and had moved to their right to pass me, I would speed off, leaving them in my smoke, satisfied that I had given them "a taste of their own medicine."

I let tailgaters who rode my bumper with high beams blazing go by, then followed their cars closely with *my* high beams on. Other tailgaters received my "quick-braking treatment." I depressed my brake pedal suddenly, forcing them to brake to avoid a collision; then at the last second I accelerated. This "punishment" served as a warning not to tailgate. Lesser offenders received hand gestures, scornful looks, mouthed obscenities, and blasts from my horn. Dr. Meyer Friedman aptly calls behavior like mine "being policeman to the world."

Beside having been a vigilante myself, I have also been the victim of other vigilantes. You may remember the incident, described earlier, when the driver of a pickup truck punished a friend and me on our way to play racquetball. The truck driver was a violent vigilante, one who would probably damage another driver's vehicle or seek a personal confrontation if he had the chance.

More recently, I had an encounter with another vigilante. I pulled up behind a car at a stoplight. It was a routine stop I'd made thousands of times on the way home from work over the last ten years. When the light changed I turned left, following the same car. Suddenly, the car ahead of me stopped abruptly. I also halted, assuming a stray animal had darted across the road. After five seconds or so, I realized there was no stray animal. The driver was punishing me—for what, I didn't know.

Annoyed, I reached for my pad to jot down the license number, but before I could, the car accelerated, spinning its wheels and roaring down the road. On reflection, I assume the driver thought my car had come too close to his at the stoplight, although my stopping distance was the same as it has been since I began driving.

This past summer I vacationed in a small town in Idaho which has a right-of-way ordinance for pedestrians. One day I walked across the street, following a mechanic I had asked to check my rented vehicle for a minor difficulty. In doing so I crossed well in front of an approaching line of cars coming along the street. The driver of the first vehicle honked his horn, rolled down his window, and shouted, "The next time you do that I'll run you over!"

Vigilante-style punishment is not always so benign. When a vigilante meets another vigilante, the result can be death. The *New York Times* recounted two such incidents in 1995–1996. In one, a vigilante chased a speeder, then forced him off the road. As he approached the speeder's car to give him a piece of his mind, the vigilante was confronted by several men in the car. They shot him dead. In another incident, a man driving his wife to work chased a driver who had cut him off; the man pulled up beside the offending driver and gave him the finger. The other driver took out a revolver and shot and killed the vigilante's wife.

Punishing drivers who put you at risk and who you believe "need to be taught a lesson" is one of the most dangerous things you can do on the road. Worse yet is retaliating when another vigilante punishes you.

Vigilante-style punishment ranges from menacing words and rude gestures to murder. But all vigilantes have one thing in common: they experience the "offense" of the other driver as being personal. They respond to traffic infractions as if they had been struck, and they want to hit back.

It's not hard to understand where this reaction originates. It is the survival instinct in all animal species—fight or flight. You can read about it in Deuteronomy: "An eye for an eye, a tooth for a tooth." You can hear it from parents when they instruct their children who complain of being hit by other children, "Hit him back!" You can view it in thousands of movie and television programs where the plot repeatedly teaches that injury can be resolved only by inflicting greater injury on the perpetrator.

The automobile advertisers are only making things worse. William Haddon, former head of the Insurance Institute for Highway Safety in Washington, D.C., was quoted in Peter Marsh and Peter Collett's *Driving Passion* on the subject of inflammatory names for autos: "There is . . . the glaring discrepancy between the need of societies to reduce motor vehicle casualties . . . and the image of violence and machismo with which many of the vehicles are sold; images which it is reasonable to believe increase the occurrence of motor vehicle death and maiming. . . ." As noted in chapter 13, Marsh and Collett call attention to the names Jaguar, Mustang, Cougar, Bronco, Panther, Taurus, Firebird, and Thunderbird—all fast and violent.

Vigilantes take what they've learned about violence and retribution to heart. I believe this accounts for the statement often heard from vigilantes that they are as much a victim as the person they injured; they were only following the advice they had been given since childhood. Vigilantes, at the time of their revenge, do not view their anger as a problem, their acts as unjustified, or the results as undeserved. (Often, this changes later, when they cool down.) This is due to the nature of anger: anger is always perceived by the angry person as justified. It only occurs when something that person holds as truth is violated.

The catch is that we all have different "truths." Believing drivers should pull over to let me pass may be my "truth"; believing that no one should drive faster than the posted speed limit may be yours. We'll both become angry, and we'll both feel justified in our anger, when other drivers violate our truths. That anger can escalate very quickly into irrational rage.

For the vigilante to resign from the self-appointed role of "policeman to the world," he or she must come to realize that all these teachings are wrong, and not applicable to most highway experiences. Just as you cannot always believe your eyes (remember the Necker cube), you cannot always believe your "logical" conclusions. For example:

- Just because you feel as though you have been personally injured doesn't mean you have been.

- Just because you conclude the offending driver is a "bad" person doesn't mean he is.

- Just because you believe it's in your best interest to hit back doesn't mean it is.

- Just because you believe the other driver will benefit from the lesson you've taught her doesn't mean she will.

- Just because you believe the incident has spoiled an otherwise pleasant journey doesn't mean it has.

Most highway vigilantes aren't vigilantes in their interactions with other people off the highway. They know the five conclusions mentioned above aren't usually true. In fact, those thoughts might not even cross their minds. Why then do people who seem perfectly reasonable behave like dark avengers when they get behind the wheel? One answer is that they don't know enough about other drivers. Clues as to the motivation and personality of the other driver are minimal. Consequently, they are guided by imagination, not facts. The way to change this is to replace imagined fears with knowledge and understanding.

How can we change our culturally reinforced punishing attitudes into positive attitudes? When we witness "bad" driving, we must replace old beliefs, attitudes, and assumptions with new ones. This is easier to do than you might think.

She's dangerous while on this turf.
Best give her a wide, wide berth.
Paying her back only escalates,
Giving her cause to fuel her hates.
Model good driving, try to teach—
Leave punishment to the police.

Installation Step 1: Discussion

The first step in changing a "Teach 'em a Lesson"
attitude to a "Leave Punishment to the Police" attitude is to discuss your reaction to other drivers
who put you at risk. Compare your reaction to the
experiences mentioned below.

Just like the scornful driver, the vigilante takes
highway events personally. The only difference is
that the vigilante carries his feeling of personal injury to the next step—revenge.

True, to some degree you may be endangered
by another driver's behavior. A tailgater poses real
risks if you have to stop suddenly. However, a
speeding car weaving from one lane to another at
some distance poses only a remote threat to you,
although such driving threatens the safety of others. In both cases, however, it's not personal; it's not
directed at you.

Does this distinction make a difference? Yes,
because if it is personal, you have much greater
reason to be on your guard, or to prepare for fight
or flight.

. . .

How do you decide whether it's personal? You can't decide solely on the basis of the pain endured; you must also evaluate the circumstances surrounding the painful experience.

For example, if you're walking in the woods and a hard object strikes your head, hurting you but neither drawing blood nor causing diminished consciousness, you first thought is likely to be, "What did that?" not "Who did that?" You think of acorns, not stones. You think of impersonal acts, not personal ones.

On the other hand, if you're walking on a battlefield in wartime, and a hard object strikes your helmet, your first thought, after running for cover, is apt to be, "Who did that?" not "What did that?" You think of personal threats (someone is trying to kill me), not impersonal ones—bullets, not acorns.

If you are a vigilante, the highway feels like a battlefield. But in reality, it's much more benign. It's not as benign as a walk in the woods, but the only drivers who personally threaten you will be vigilantes, and they will not actually threaten your life unless you take vigilante-style action yourself.

Your stress level will be much lower if you remember that bad driving by others is not directed at you personally. Expect to see all degrees of driving skill. Expect to see instances of bad judgment. That's just our highway world.

"Bad drivers are bad people." This is another belief that vigilantes hold dear. But most "bad" drivers look pretty much like you and me! In the movie *The Wizard of Oz* there is a scene in the Emerald City in which Dorothy confronts the bumbling "wizard," who is hiding behind the curtain, and scolds him, "You're a *bad* man!"

The stammering wizard replies, "No, I'm a good man—just a very bad wizard!"

Most bad drivers are good men and women. They are just guilty of some bad driving.

Moreover, most "bad" drivers' motives are not reprehensible. In fact, practically all of them regard their motives as virtuous. A speeding driver is probably trying to be on time for an appointment. A slow driver may be old and driving cautiously. Someone who cuts you off may believe she had to make a quick decision.

Yes, it is bad driving. Yes, it is poor judgment. But it is not malicious. The driver's "misdeed" was not the product of evil, destined to proliferate if not stopped.

You are more likely to enjoy your driving if you believe: "They probably have a good reason. Or maybe they just made a mistake. I might drive that way myself in similar circumstances. The situation would be understandable if I just knew the facts."

Giving most drivers the benefit of the doubt will not compromise your ability to recognize the minority of drivers who not only drive badly but are bad people.

It's true that certain drivers, if given a chance, would rob, hurt, and even kill. Others, high on drugs or alcohol, might crash into you. Stupid or impaired drivers could wreck your car through negligence or bad judgment.

These are, however, a minority, and the wise response if you encounter them is not to seek revenge, but to give them wide berth—flight, not fight.

"Don't let them get away with it—it's my duty to hit back." Vigilantes believe that they have a duty to teach the bad driver a lesson. However, if you no longer regard the bad driving you witnessed as directed at you personally, or as the deed of a malicious person, what purpose does it serve for you to punish the driver?

By punishment, I mean intentional acts of retaliation beyond quickly honking your horn. I refer to some act of retribution that penalizes, humiliates, or injures the other driver.

These can range from several blasts of the horn to shouting, swearing, gesturing, and grimacing, and up to personal confrontation and physical injury. Even a curse uttered within the confines of your own car, which the other driver will never hear, is similarly motivated to make the offender "pay" for his offense.

While you can make the case for moral obligation to go to the aid of a person being mugged, it's harder to justify punishing an aggressive driver for tailgating or a blocker for driving slowly. Unlike the mugger, the slow driver does not perceive her driving as "bad." She may believe she is within her rights, driving within the speed limit.

Indeed, she could easily think that the vigilante's driving is bad. He's a madman, endangering her comfort and safety! What the vigilante intended as punishment could be perceived as an unprovoked attack. In this way, the vigilante becomes the other driver's "bad" driver.

By punishing, the vigilante escalates his own anger and the anger of the other drivers, thus raising the level of hostility that pollutes our nation's highways.

If you really wish to aid the police, jot down the offender's license number and send it with details to appropriate authorities. That would make sense, and it would show you're serious. Ask yourself whether your desire to punish is based on morality or on revenge, a desire to retaliate by venting your spleen on the "bad" person. The vigilante as policeman, judge, and executioner was outlawed long ago in civilized countries.

Many states have started call-in numbers for cell phone users. Maryland was one of the first. Motorists seeing an aggressive driver or other non-emergency event can call #77 and talk to a police officer who can radio a state trooper in the vicinity to investigate. This kind of reporting really does work.

I gave up my "six-guns" long ago and retired from my role as policeman to the world. It's far better to leave punishment to the police. I now believe that it's not my business to punish.

"Punishment will teach them a lesson—if you let them get away with it, their driving will get worse." Does vigilante punishment improve driving skills by causing drivers to think twice about what they are doing? I doubt it. It doesn't make sense to believe that an adult who is convinced he is in the right will let abuse from another driver convince him otherwise.

Advocates of punishment disagree. They point not only to parental use of punishment to curb unacceptable behavior in children, but to the legal system's use of police and jails as punishment to deter lawbreaking. Doesn't it stand to reason, they argue, that if we all punished bad drivers, highway manners would improve?

Again, I doubt it. Parents and police are culturally identified and culturally sanctioned authorities. Punishment, when it comes from someone other than a socially sanctioned punisher, is not perceived as punishment at all, but as "sticking your nose in someone else's business."

Even as children, we defy baby-sitters with the shout, "You're not my mother!" And, as adults, if our peers reprimand us for something, our reply might be to suggest someplace they could "stick it"! Authoritarian personalities without a badge or proper credentials have little effect in making discipline stick.

Remember, instead, that experience is the best teacher. By being the best driver you can be, you give the errant driver a model to learn from. Modeling is a far better teacher than punishment. Choose to model good driving. You'll be far more effective, and you'll make your journey more pleasant.

"Bad drivers spoil my trip." This final belief of the vigilante can come about only if you let it. If you overreact to every misdeed you see on the highway, blast the other driver, and curse about the event over and over again to your passengers, you spoil your journey and that of everyone else in your vehicle. If you downplay the event, treating it as just another problem to be solved, it will gradually fade in your awareness until it reaches proper proportions.

Since I gave up the vigilante business, my life on the road has been much more pleasant, peaceful, and relaxed. My passengers are extremely grateful. Now we talk and laugh and play.

Further, I've noticed no deterioration in the driving expertise of other drivers since I retired from punishing. Indeed, quite the contrary. Other drivers now seem more courteous, and quite adept.

I wonder: Could I have been the problem?

Installation Step 2: Attitude Change Card

As with other driving styles, you'll need help in practicing your new beliefs. Once again, put the opposing points of view on opposite sides of an index card. On one side write your old beliefs, which need to be reviewed, but not memorized.

Old Beliefs

Stressor: A "bad" driver
Urge: To punish
Statements: Teach him a lesson
                 Give her a taste of her own medicine
                 Don't let him get away with it
                 She's a bad person
                 He'll spoil my trip

On the other side, write the alternative new attitude. Since you will be memorizing your new beliefs, you can choose whether to write them in the form of statements or a poem:

New Beliefs

Stressor:	Driver endangering me or others
Urge:	To problem-solve
Statements:	They may not be playing with a full deck
	Best to give them wide berth
	My punishing only aggravates
	Model good driving
	Leave punishment to the police
Poem:	She's dangerous while on this turf.
	Best give her a wide, wide berth.
	Paying her back only escalates,
	Giving her cause to fuel her hates.
	Model good driving, try to teach—
	Leave punishment to the police.

Installation Step 3: Memorize

To make the new belief your own, you must come to know it by heart. The best way is through active memorization. Memorize the "New Beliefs" side of your Attitude Change Card. Memorize both the triggering event, "When another driver puts me at risk," and the new belief, "Then I say to myself . . ."

Carry the card with you when you drive; review it before starting out. Once you've identified the old belief and memorized the new belief, the new belief will kick in automatically without conscious effort on your part.

Installation Step 4: Debate

Using the Attitude Change Card to guide you, debate a friend, taking turns on the belief you advocate. Continue until you can be equally convincing on either side. It might go like this:

JOHN (*for "Teach 'em a Lesson"*). You wouldn't believe what happened the other day. Someone wouldn't let me go by. He was blocking me and I drove up on his bumper really close. I was going to teach him a lesson on what happens to him when he does that kind of thing. Then I decided to get in front of him and put on my brakes. Give him a taste of his own medicine, I say; don't let him get away with it. Most of them are evil, they are enemies, and the only way they are going to learn is to have their head knocked in a little bit, you know? Make them pay. That is the only way people learn anyhow. You have to knock some sense into their heads. That's my duty as a citizen. The police are not there, they are not doing it, so I'm going to do it."

CAROL (*for "Leave Punishment to the Police"*). "John, do you really think that punishing someone is going to teach them anything? They are not looking to you for lessons on how to drive. If you want to teach them something, you could try modeling good driving, which is something you obviously are not doing. More important, the people you are punishing could be armed; you could easily end up dead. The next thing you know, you guys are into something that you can't get out of so easily. It is not safe and doesn't make any sense and it doesn't even work. Try modeling good driving; forget about what other people are doing and leave punishment to the police.

Then change sides.

CAROL   (*for "Teach 'em a Lesson"*). What am I supposed to do if somebody is driving dangerously? It is my duty to point out to them that that is no way to drive. They should pay for that kind of behavior. Give them a taste of their own medicine. These people need me to teach them a lesson. Block them or tailgate them a little bit—what is so bad about that? Its not going to lead to anything. The main thing is that they get a sense of what they are not supposed to do and then they will back off and that will be the end of it.

JOHN   (*for "Leave Punishment to the Police"*). "Hey, open up your eyes. This is the real world, not a game of cowboys-and-Indians. Those people in the other car may not be playing with a full deck and you might end up with your brains blown out. I think it is much better to give them wide berth; if they are risky, keep away from them. Punishing is only going to aggravate them. When you start knocking them around they are going to fight back. What I found that really works for me is to model good driving. I'm a good driver. I think that teaches people better than anything else; they look at me and say, 'That guy knows how to drive, maybe I can drive like that.' I leave punishment to the police, because it isn't my business. I have a lot of other things that I like to do in my car besides punishing other people.

Installation Step 5: Relaxation Exercise

Reserve fifteen minutes for yourself. Pick a quiet spot, where you won't be disturbed. Elicit the relaxation response described in chapter 11 by taking a few slow, deep breaths, inhaling to the count of five, and exhaling more and more slowly to the counts of five, ten, fifteen, and twenty. Take your Attitude Change Card, and proceed as follows:

- Elicit the relaxation response.

- Visualize or imagine another driver putting you at risk.

- Read your list of new beliefs.

- Once again, elicit the relaxation response.

- Visualize or imagine another driver putting you at risk.

- Read your list of new beliefs.

- Try to remember them.

- Elicit the relaxation response one more time.

Installation Step 6: Practice!

Imagine you are driving in the middle lane of a highway when someone abruptly cuts in front of you from the left, forcing you to apply your brakes. Then he speeds on, making another lane change to gain more ground, cutting in front of another vehicle up ahead. You say:

"No need to punish, leave that to the police. He's probably a good person, rushing to be on time, trying to keep his commitments. Let's give that driver a wide berth."

It's not always easy to do. Memorizing your new beliefs is important, along with practice. The combination will dissipate most of your rage and allow you to turn your attention away from the person who cut you off, and back to enjoying the road.

Every time you encounter a driver who you believe is putting you or someone else at risk, read this jingle, or have a friend read it to you.

Vigilante's Jingle

Gil shook his fist at Jill.
Jill gave the finger to Phil.
Phil yelled a bad name at Bill.
And so goes the dance of ill-will.

Leave punishment to the police.

PART THREE

THE ROAD TO HEALTH

No psychic value can disappear without being replaced by another of equal intensity.

—Carl Gustav Jung

Drivers holding the five stressful driving beliefs that have been the primary focus of this book have a grossly exaggerated sense of *mistrust= threat=danger*; their highway world abounds with rudeness and nastiness.

These attitudes can be changed without impairing your ability to drive your car skillfully. On the contrary, changing the attitudes will increase your ability to operate your vehicle both skillfully and safely. You won't be so distracted, impatient, or impulsive.

What's more, when you make the changes, you will experience the highway world as a better place. It's an amazing experience when you first drive in this friendlier, more courteous world. It seems too good to be true.

We move from a world of danger and threat into a world of opportunity and beauty when we decide to change these attitudes. By deciding to focus on making time good, in place of making good time, we remove a consideration that will cloud our whole driving experience and replace it with a determination to maximize enjoyment. We are guaranteed enhanced self-esteem when we focus on treating ourselves royally in place of making up competitions with others. By developing a compassionate attitude toward others on the road, giving them the benefit of the doubt, letting them live and let live, and leaving punishment to the police, we free our energies for living life fully.

Crossing over from the warpath to the beauty path requires not only changing these beliefs cognitively, but coming to hold them with conviction, to really take them to heart. How do you develop conviction? Changing your attitudes and embracing new points of view can come about through the following five procedures.

First: Change everything you can that bears on the polarity *mistrust=threat=danger* versus *trust= friend=safe* by making use of your Attitude Change Cards: that means working on all five stressful driving beliefs simultaneously. A little bit of each one every day. Why is it important to work on all five at once? Because they're all linked and they reinforce one another.

It's really no different from improving your tennis game. Hitting the ball can't be learned in isolation. You need to learn how to plant your feet, hold the racquet, watch the ball, and so on.

Remember, the neurons in the brain either fire or they don't fire. Neurons receive either excitatory signals or inhibitory signals. The vigor of the response of any set of neurons to a given stimulus is determined by the number of neurons in the set that are stimulated enough to fire. If only half the members of the team are motivated to play, the total team's effort will be halved. Similarly, how angry you get is determined by how many of the neurons in that particular set are stimulated enough to fire.

Since all five attitudes contribute to the *mistrust=threat=danger* versus *trust=friend=safe* polarity, the more you change to positive driving attitudes, the fewer "anger" neurons fire, and the better you feel.

•   •   •

Second: Memorize! In order to hold the new beliefs with conviction, you must convert them from short-term memory to long-term memory. That way they really, indeed literally, become part of you: new brain neuronal connections take place and your gray matter grows. Read the new beliefs each morning soon after awakening and before you drive off, and then again before going to sleep, imagining situations where they are relevant. This takes only a few minutes.

You know the names attached to the five driving attitudes. Without looking at your Attitude Change Cards, try to recall the new beliefs you need to change to. Note how many lines of each "new belief" poem you remembered, then look at the cards, refresh your memory, put the cards away, and try to recall again. Repeat this three times each day with each card. This will take less than five minutes. In time, you will remember them all. Think of the number of people's names you remember with no difficulty. What makes it seem hard to memorize these new beliefs is not that they are so difficult to memorize, it's that you are resisting changing your point of view.

It is not possible to memorize these new beliefs and not change!

Third: Practice, practice, practice. Reread the new beliefs and try to remember them each time you slip back into the old attitudes, bringing them into play at the appropriate time. In learning how to improve your tennis game, you might ask a pro to help you. He watches you play, and at a certain point he may say, "No, not that way, do it this way." You go back over the stroke with the new belief in mind.

Don't be hard on yourself if you have trouble learning or if you keep forgetting. Don't give up if after an initial improvement you have a day when you revert back to Mr. Hyde. Be patient with yourself.

Fourth: Incorporate the new beliefs by precise timing. You learn a new sequence of thoughts to replace the old ones. In tennis the eye of the tennis player sees the ball, the brain calculates the distance and at a certain point initiates the new thought, then the swing. The eye of the stressed driver sees the stressful driving event, "Rude driver cutting me off," and at the appropriate moment initiates the new thought, "Be my guest," and then the new driving behavior, "Let him in."

What is the appropriate moment? The timing should occur as close as possible to when your old way of thinking is about to trigger the stress response: just as the rude driver is about to cut in front of you. At that point the new thoughts rush in, the stress response is thwarted, the new response kicks in, and you let him cut in.

When you find yourself erupting in the old manner, ask yourself which set of values was involved. Were you trying to make good time, or trying to beat someone? Or had you just decided you didn't like something about the other guy? At that point, go over the pertinent new set of beliefs. Try to memorize them right on the spot, then again an hour after you arrive home and have had time to cool down. Make a special point of reviewing the new beliefs that night before going to bed, and the next morning before setting off.

It is essential to put the relevant card in a prominent place on your dashboard where you can easily keep it in view.

Fifth: Persist! Within a month, if you are persistent in your practice, you will notice a shift toward the new world, and by three months you won't go back (except for brief occasional lapses).

You will find it easier to put it all together if you learn a relaxation technique. I suggest a simple yet effective one in chapter 11. I also recommend the relaxation techniques of Jon Kabot-Zinn and Herbert Benson. Shifting from the old beliefs to the new beliefs is much easier if you practice while in an altered state of consciousness brought about through a simple relaxation, breathing, and focusing exercise.

It's similar to shifting the gears of a car. In order to go from one gear to the next, the transmission must be placed in neutral by engaging the clutch. Only then can you move easily to another gear.

The relaxation response fulfills the same function as the clutch when it comes to shifting values. You must stop being driven by one before you can begin moving to another. Most of the time, we race from our work to our cars. Then we race to our homes, where we race through our chores, running by with hardly a glance at our spouses, children, and friends. We only disengage on vacation, and then it takes three to eight days to slow down and adopt another way of going through the day. The relaxation response is a skill that allows you to disengage anytime you have five to fifteen minutes to devote to it. Even though the time is short, contemplating new beliefs during this period increases the rate at which the old undesirable "passengers" get out of the car and the new companions get in.

Try it! Reserve fifteen minutes for yourself. Pick a quiet spot, where you won't be disturbed. Take your five cards, and proceed as follows. Suppose you want to reduce your overreaction to tailgaters:

- Elicit the relaxation response.

- Visualize or imagine a tailgater.

- Read your list of new beliefs.

- Once again, elicit the relaxation response.

- Visualize or imagine the tailgater.

- Read your list of new beliefs.

- Try to remember them.

- Elicit the relaxation response one more time.

Doing this with each highway stressor you overreact to will gradually extinguish your hostility. It's that simple.

Gradually, pleasurable highway attitudes will begin to take hold. These, too, will become intertwined and mutually reinforcing. You'll drive to make time good and treat yourself and your passengers like number one beings. Delays are no longer a problem. On the contrary, delays become opportunities to further relax your vigilance and concentrate on pleasurable experiences. You'll find yourself courteous and considerate of other vehicles needing to pass.

Learning new driving attitudes is no different from acquiring any new skill. Study, memorize, and practice until you incorporate the knowledge. With time, the new attitudes will feel familiar and will be a source of self-esteem.

Your automobile will become a "port in the storm."

"I've never unclasped a seat belt from around a corpse," one police officer remarked. That's because people wearing seat belts die in crashes much less often than people who aren't wearing them. In Massachusetts in 1992, nine out of every ten traffic fatalities involved individuals not wearing seat belts. If there's one thing that's been proven in driving safety, it's that seat belts save lives. It's undisputed. Yet many of us don't wear them. Why?

The paradoxical answer is that people want the risk; it makes us feel more alive. Just as people choose to ride roller coasters or make free-fall parachute jumps, when driving they court the increased possibility of death to gain a heightened experience of being alive. Consequently, trying to get people to wear seat belts by emphasizing risk is like trying to persuade someone to avoid parachute jumping because she might get killed.

All of the beliefs that contribute to aggressive driving and highway anger increase the risk of injury and death. Trying to scare people into changing their beliefs would be fruitless—"Try and Make Me."

It is also true that if individuals have no other way to feel more alive except to escalate risky driving, then they're going to gradually increase the risk level, because as soon as they master one risk level they will feel bored and numb unless they further escalate the degree of risk. Thus the way to get individuals to wear seat belts is to teach them another way of feeling alive besides taking risks. This other way is contained in the five alternative beliefs that form the core of this book. How it works is best illustrated by telling you about our experience with eleven teenagers.

We asked the teenagers in our Larson Driver Attitude Change Seminar how many of them wore their seat belts every time they drove. Roughly half responded that they did. Our group reflected the national average, since surveys show that fewer than 50 percent of people riding in cars use seat belts. The answer given by the other half of the teenagers ranged from never wearing a seat belt to once-in-a-while to wearing one about 50 percent of the time. When asked why they didn't wear seat belts, they gave vague answers: "I don't know." "I don't feel like it." "I don't think about it when I get into the car."

At first we were perplexed. What was going on? There must be more to "I don't feel like it" and "I don't think about it." As we pondered those responses, we began to see the five stressful driver attitudes lurking in the background.

"I don't think about it when I get into the car" translates into "I didn't want to take the time." This negligent disregard for safety is in part a product of "Make Good Time." The driver preoccupied with making good time doesn't want to take the time required for the act of buckling. The driver believes, "It takes too long."

While this may sound ridiculous, it is true. I've treated many drivers who were so concerned with making good time that they wouldn't take the time for a visit to the bathroom and would argue vehemently on the importance of toilet paper being put on the roll so that the paper comes over the top rather than down the back because it saves time that way. I've seen two men almost come to blows over a debate about which method of hanging toilet paper was proper!

As you begin to shift your attitude from "Make Good Time" to "Make Time Good," you will plan your travel with time to spare. This new attitude will certainly allow you to plan for the three seconds it takes to buckle your seat belt. The three seconds are not the only issue. People determined to make good time place time ahead of safety. They think, "How can I make good time on this trip?" "By buckling my seat belt" is not the natural answer to that question.

Once you start placing safety and enjoyment ahead of time, then it follows naturally that you will be more likely to buckle up. Your first thought will be, "How can I make this ride safe and pleasant for myself and my passengers?" Buckling everyone's seat belt is an easy place to start.

We never told the teenagers to wear their seat belts. Yet during follow-up testing we were thrilled to discover that of the teenagers who didn't already wear their seat belts 100 percent of the time, seat belt use went up from an average of 50 percent of the time to an average of 75 percent of the time. Think of the lives that could be saved and the injuries that could be avoided if the national average could be increased that much.

I repeat, we never told the teenagers to wear their seat belts. They had to figure out for themselves that wearing seat belts would enhance their safety and their enjoyment. How would it enhance their enjoyment? Remember the two ways of getting self-esteem? The first way, by setting goals, such as making good time, and striving to achieve them focuses on the end result of getting there in record time, not on enjoying your time in the car. The second way of getting self-esteem, by enjoying yourself and your relationships, is part of learning the new attitude of "Make Time Good." Your focus shifts not only to allowing extra time, but to valuing your time in the car and planning to make it as much fun as it can be. I believe that the heightened sense of value the teenagers felt toward their own lives is what made them more likely to buckle up.

Next, we took a look at the "I don't feel like it" response. Could always wanting to be number one influence buckling or not buckling that belt? The most competitive drivers at our seminar for teenagers expressed the typical "Be Number One" beliefs in statements such as "No one passes me," "I always want to be first," or "I have to be in front, and I get angry when someone passes me." I believe that this "king of the road" attitude contributes to a sense of being above other people and above the rules of the road.

It makes sense that as their attitude shifted from the goal-oriented "Be Number One" to the enhanced pleasure- and relationship-oriented "Be a Number One Being," their sense of being above the rules would also shift to placing greater value on their enjoyment. You can't enjoy your life if you're dead or injured, so buckling up follows naturally.

"Try and make me," says the blocker. You can certainly hear the attitude coming across in this driver belief. The response "I don't feel like putting on my seat belt" could easily have the undertone, "and you can't make me." How many times have drivers, especially young drivers, been told to wear their seat belts? Between parent pleas, driving instructor warnings, and classroom "scare statistics," they should be thoroughly convinced that wearing their seat belts could save their lives. They are convinced, but they still don't wear them. With all the safety instruction American drivers have gone through, the fact that only half of us are wearing seat belts is the best proof that more seat belt safety instruction won't do any good. What is needed is a shift from a "Try and Make Me" attitude to a more positive "Be My Guest" attitude.

This works because what is really changing, once again, is how the driver gets self-esteem. The "Try and Make Me" driver gets it from not being forced to do what he doesn't want to do, in this case, move over. He thinks, "You can't make me move over, and you can't make me do *anything*, including buckle my seat belt."

Compare that to the "Be My Guest" way of getting self-esteem, through choosing to be courteous. The choice is now his to treat others with kindness and consideration, as if they were guests in his home. No one is forcing him to do this; he wants to do it. He is also now free to choose to buckle his seat belt. No one is forcing him to do that either.

What about "They Shouldn't Be Allowed"? Does that attitude creep in somehow? Could the response "I don't feel like it" really be saying, "and I don't have to because the rules are made for average people who need them, not for me." "They Shouldn't Be Allowed" is an attitude of superiority, deriving self-esteem from feeling better than those perceived as inferior. Once you see yourself as a superior driver, it's easy to think, "The rules don't apply to me the same way they apply to those lesser folk." Self-esteem comes from constantly comparing yourself to others and coming out on top.

The minute you make the shift to "Live and Let Live," your entire focus changes to accepting others as they are. We all have our idiosyncrasies. Now self-esteem comes from accepting diversity and having positive regard for yourself as well as for others. This egalitarian attitude leads to the conscious or unconscious conclusion that, if we're all more or less equal, then maybe the rules apply equally to everyone, including me.

Finally, is "Teach 'em a Lesson" operating in deciding not to wear a seat belt? The driver with this attitude gets self-esteem from making the rules and enforcing them. What he says, goes. People who make the rules often believe that they are above them.

The shift to "Leave Punishment to the Police" takes the rule-making task away from this driver. Since the police are now making the rules, I had better follow them like everyone else. And since self-esteem is now derived from modeling good driving, what better way to model good driving than to wear my seat belt?

Why don't you wear your seat belt? "I don't know" means "I'm not aware of how the way I'm getting self-esteem on the road is interfering with my natural desire for self-preservation." As each of the five stressful driving attitudes is replaced by its positive alternative, internal beliefs and external strategies change from destructive to life-enhancing ways of getting self-esteem: from not buckling, to buckling.

Anger blows out the lamp of the mind.
—*Robert Green Ingersoll*

Dr. Ronald Turco, a psychiatrist who works part-time as a detective with the Newburgh, New York, Police Department, said, "I'm just extremely cautious when I'm driving. When somebody cuts me off, I just let them go because they could pull out a gun. I don't argue with anybody. It's too crazy. It used to be, years ago, you could shake a fist and let some steam off, but now you can't."

Is that what you'd do? Long after your own highway anger has diminished, you can still be enraged anew by another driver's fury at you. It's understandable that rage in another person triggers an alarm reaction in you—the person wants to harm you in some way. Remember the Anger Intensity Scale in chapter 6? It showed how a person's anger can be ranked from zero (contentment) to ten (killing rage). The scale told us that if another driver's anger is noticeable from his automobile, it's at least at a seven. Chances are you're dealing with a vigilante who believes you deserve punishment and is driving his car in a way to inflict it. Since you don't know to what lengths he is prepared to go, you automatically become aroused, vigilant, and ready for fight or flight. True, he may be getting ready only to mouth an obscenity or give you the finger, but you don't know; he might have a gun.

A 1987 study of 137 Los Angeles highway firearm assaults identified as most common the following precipitating events: tailgating, impeding traffic, and merging or lane changing. In this chapter, I suggest attitudes and strategies for you to use when you are confronted by these three highway events. But first, some general principles:

- Accept the fact that you're bound to meet a vigilante someday. That way you will be less affronted when it happens.

- Don't take it personally. Although it feels personal, it's not you the angry driver is mad at. It could be anybody this driver thinks is obstructing what he or she wants to do.

- Play it down. Stay cool. Don't make it a big deal.

- Remember, in most cases the angry driver is not truly dangerous and will not physically harm you, especially if you don't escalate and retaliate.

- There may be a good reason he or she is driving this way.

- Recall Ingersoll's words: "Anger blows out the lamp of the mind." That other person is not playing with a full deck.

- View this driver as desperate and anxious, not as a challenger. Give him or her wide berth. The highway is not the place for petty squabbles.

- Avoid eye contact; that keeps it impersonal.

- If he or she escalates, get out of there. This driver may be dangerous. Go for help; find a police officer.

Now, on to the specifics.

TAILGATING

Tailgating is dangerous! One morning, on my commute into New York during rush hour, I saw in my rearview mirror that a car was approaching rapidly. The driver flashed her lights several times and tailgated me, obviously in a desperate hurry. I had an opportunity to pull over into the middle lane and did just that. As she sped by, hard on her heels was another tailgater, and after that car, yet another, and after that a fourth and a fifth. They moved as a unit, each one pushing the one in front, scarcely two feet apart. Zip—zip—zip—zip—zip.

A few minutes later, as I approached the neighborhood of Yankee Stadium, the traffic became congested and slowed to a crawl. The far left lane was completely stopped, and all of us had to squeeze into the two right lanes. Soon the cause for the obstruction came into view: the five tailgaters had run into each other when the lead vehicle braked suddenly to avoid hitting a car that swerved in front of her. Crash—crash—crash—crash!

The presence of real imminent danger distinguishes tailgating from other highway stressors. Multivehicle accidents are common. Unaware of the danger, the tailgater is singularly focused on speeding to his or her destination. Often, the tailgater is a victim of an illusion created by a feeling of "safety in numbers." "Everybody" seems to be speeding; it's the thing to do. "Come on gang, let's pass those dawdlers!"

.   .   .

In addition to finding tailgaters on high-speed ex-
pressways, you are apt to encounter them in two
other circumstances: on two-lane roads and when
slowing down to make a turn. On high-speed ex-
pressways and two-lane roads, the tailgaters are
speeding to make good time; in the last instance,
when you make a turn, even slow drivers may inadvertently become tailgaters.

The sense of alarm you feel with a tailgater
comes from more than just the real danger. You
also can sense the tailgater's mood. A perceptive
driver can tell the difference between the driver
who simply wants to pass and the hostile tailgater.
How a driver flashes his lights, blows his horn, or
approaches you conveys his emotional state. Some
"ask" to pass, some "expect" to pass, some "insist"
on passing, and some desperately "demand" to
pass—"or else!"

It's helpful in managing your emotions to think
of the tailgater as a person who is being transformed from a kindly Dr. Jekyll, speeding along to
his destination, to a dangerous Mr. Hyde. The self-
esteem of a well-intentioned Dr. Jekyll is dependent
on achieving certain driving goals, usually to reach
a destination by a set time or to maintain a certain
speed. Failure to achieve these goals (your vehicle
is his obstacle) threatens his self-esteem, producing
a painfully depressed mood. Since he deems you
and your car responsible for the bad driving that
hinders him from meeting his goals, he regards you
as beneath contempt. Finally, Mr. Hyde seeks a
method to punish you, to make your life miserable.
The longer he has to wait, the more his rage mixes
with mounting desperation.

It's this combination of desperation and anger
in tailgaters, together with your own awareness of

real risk, that can cause you to feel both anger and fear. Should you fight or flee? When you can't decide, you feel overwhelmed and slightly confused. What should you do?

1. Don't look at the tailgater or his car. Ordinarily you would look behind and keep an eye on danger, but in this case you're safer not to. Usually, tailgaters are competent drivers, so you don't have to watch them like a hawk. By avoiding eye contact, you'll make it less personal for both of you, and without that element of personal challenge you'll be calmer and more in control of your car. I adjust my rearview mirror so I can see at a glance the right half of the car behind me but I cannot see the driver's face (nor can he see mine).

2. Don't speed up or slow down. Drive like a state trooper: real steady. If the way you drive your car is not affected by his presence, he is more apt to calm down. Or, realizing that he cannot influence you, he'll pass you on the right. If there's room, you should pull over. If he senses any fear or panic on your part, he will press harder. If he senses that you're going to fight him, he'll rise to the challenge.

3. Concentrate on driving your car and, when it is safe to do so, pull over and let him pass. He wants to go faster than you do, so let him. If you can't pull over immediately, turn on your right rear directional signal to let him know you will pull over when it's safe. This may be hard for you to do graciously if you resent his rudeness.

You may be tempted to punish him by denying him the right-of-way. It will be easier if you consider that more than likely there is a good reason he wants to pass. He may be trying to keep an urgent appointment. Since he represents a danger to you, give him a wide berth. Don't let his rudeness erode your courtesy. Say, "Be my guest!" and give him the road. Even "bad guys" have a right to pass. Move over!

You also may have difficulty yielding the right-of-way if you perceive the driver's challenging manner as a personal threat to your self-esteem. But it's important to see him or her as desperate rather than menacing. He or she is more like a cornered animal than a schoolyard bully. Since cornered animals can inflict serious damage, your attitude and response should be different than it would be to a schoolyard bully. Bullies respect you more if you stand up to them; cornered animals, treated aggressively, just become more desperate.

Under these circumstances, a firm, cautious, no-nonsense attitude is more effective. You carefully make it possible for the animal to go free without hurting it or yourself. Remember:

- This is a trivial matter.

- It's not worth dying for.

- Use your energies elsewhere.

- Choose better battles, not this one.

• • •

But what about those situations where you can't pull over, such as when you're making a turn, or driving on a busy two-lane road?

In the first case, you're slowing to make a turn, but the car behind you keeps coming on. You instinctively hesitate to apply the brakes too strongly for fear the driver won't be able to stop, and a collision will result. However, by not slowing down you risk making your turn much too fast, and the resulting too-wide turn may cause you to collide with another car.

Anyone who drives so closely behind another vehicle that he cannot stop or swerve in an emergency loses some measure of his sensitivity, compassion, and good judgment. A sensitive, aware person will slow down and back off when his vehicle comes too close to another. However, if a diligent driver is surprised by a vehicle that suddenly slows down in front of him, bringing the two vehicles too close, fear may cause this normally courteous driver to lash out.

If you want to make a turn and there are vehicles close behind you, it is essential that you give them plenty of warning and convey to them that you are a flesh-and-blood human being with aspirations of your own, not just an inanimate obstacle. Your messages must say: I'm for real; I'm going to make a turn; I'm troubled by your closeness; I wish you'd back off; and I'm determined to make a safe turn.

Here's how to send these messages:

1. Put your turn indicator on far in advance of where you intend to turn. That gives plenty of time for the message to register.

2. Slow down far in advance of where you want to make the turn. You want to over-come potential insensitivity, so start early and avoid surprises.

3. Adjust your rearview mirror if the driver behind you continues to be too close. This will be enough to cause 50 per-cent of inadvertent tailgaters to slow down. The tailgater trying to make good time will read your mood from the way you adjust your mirror.

4. Avoid eye contact; don't speed up. Make yourself concentrate on your driving.

5. Continue to depress your brake pedal just enough to light up your tail lights, so you can control your slowing without com-ing to a crawl as you approach your corner.

6. If the driver continues to be close, roll down your window and use an arm signal (not a finger signal).

7. Concentrate on making the best turn you've ever made in your life. Vigilantes may roar around you at the last minute, and some may blow their horns, but that's their problem, not yours. Most drivers will be courteous if you follow these steps.

A second situation where it's difficult to allow a tailgater to pass is on a busy two-lane road. Here, either oncoming traffic or the absence of a sufficient straightaway precludes an impatient tailgater from passing. Nonetheless, she persists in driving too close.

Usually, the steps I've described up to now will be sufficient to curb your anxiety or anger. Both you and the tailgater are seemingly trapped by circumstance. If you can live with it, and send her the messages mentioned above, she may calm down and resign herself to being late.

However, if she persists and continues to press, assume she has a good reason. Pull over to the side of the road and wave her by. Your own journey will be much more pleasant. It's no big deal.

Believe it or not, there is a place where tailgaters have the right-of-way. On St. John Island in the Caribbean, the roads have two lanes, very winding and hilly, with virtually no straightaways. As a consequence, the law states that if someone wants to pass, you must pull off the road and let him.

Under these circumstances, tailgaters are more patient; they know you will pull over when it's safe, so they are less desperate and pushy. Likewise, for the person who pulls over there is no loss of face; he's simply being law-abiding. You can adopt the same attitude even though you're not in the Virgin Islands. Pull over and let the tailgater pass as soon as it's safe to do so.

THE BLOCKER

The blocker can be as hostile as the tailgater. One of the sweetest little old ladies you can imagine complained to me about the vicious tailgaters who made her life miserable on a daily basis. Initially, I was sympathetic, but when I became puzzled by the number of tailgaters she found on the highway, I asked her to describe her experience in more detail.

It turned out that she drove at *30 mph*! A character right out of *Arsenic and Old Lace*, she couldn't understand why drivers were perturbed by her safe driving.

You often encounter slow drivers who refuse to yield the right-of-way and let you pass, even though there are no vehicles stopping them from pulling over. Understanding which of the five stressful driver attitudes they hold helps you to devise an approach that keeps your own frustration at a minimum.

"Make Good Time": Naturally, if the driver who is blocking you is speeding to make good time, it means that you are speeding, too. If you come up behind him, wait patiently until he can pull over into an open lane. Usually, he's driving very fast anyway and will go even faster with you urging him on. He doesn't want to decrease his rate of travel, however, and will not yield the right-of-way until he can do so without slowing down. Then after he allows you to pass, he'll return to the passing lane behind your car, increase his speed, and you both will go whizzing along.

"Be Number One": In the case of the driver who is competing to be number one (which of course you won't know until he shows his colors), approach from behind slowly but steadily, so he doesn't feel you have a personal investment in besting him. Be patient. If he doesn't feel you're in a contest, courtesy may prevail and he'll yield. Failing this, flashing your lights may get him to go faster. He may decide to compete with you by staying ahead. In order to "beat" you, he may increase his speed, thereby accomplishing your objective of traveling faster, without your having to pass.

"Try and Make Me": If you approach slowly, in all cases, you'll confront fewer frustrating situations. In the case of the blocker, be patient and respectful as you pull up behind her. After a while, you'll become familiar to her, and if you seem like a "nice guy" she'll let you go by. Flashing your lights, honking your horn, or tailgating may cause her to become more intransigent, or even to slow down in order to frustrate you more. Rather than continuing to press and getting into a protracted struggle, simply pass on the right. When you do pass, do it decisively and quickly so that there's no chance for a contest. If you pass too gradually, she may gradually increase her speed as well.

"They Shouldn't Be Allowed": The scornful driver's arrogance and feelings of entitlement render him unable to accommodate the needs of others. It's best to simply pass on the right. It's not worth the struggle.

"Teach 'em a Lesson": The particular type of vigilante who refuses to yield the right-of-way is one I call the Policeman. If the posted speed is 55, then he is going to go 55 in the left lane, and he's going to make *sure* that no one breaks the law. Signal once with your lights that you want to pass, but be patient and don't press. Even drop back a bit. Act law-abiding! Going up a hill, he may slow down and pull over. However, if there is no reason for him to slow down, you're in for a long speed-limit ride. Once it's clear to you that you're dealing with a Policeman, either relax and tag along, or pass on the right. He ain't going to budge!

Merging or lane changing brings out the hostility in many drivers. You are especially likely to encounter an angry driver at tollbooth lines, either cutting in or trying to keep you from cutting in, entering an expressway, changing lanes on an expressway, and when two lanes merge into one.

"Chicken" is the most common game played on highways, and in most circumstances, it is played when one vehicle tries to enter a moving line of traffic. As long as skilled drivers play fair, take turns, and exercise courtesy, there is little problem. But the hostile driver who does not want to take turns or play fair creates a real danger. How should you contend with the driver trying to cut in ahead of her turn, or the driver who won't let you in?

Remember that a crash can happen in a split second in these circumstances, so be especially alert and prepared when you enter an expressway, change lanes, or merge with another lane. These are high-risk situations. Don't treat them casually. They require your most skillful driving. Stay alert: you can never predict what will happen.

Confrontations may occur, but because of the extreme danger of an accident, adopt the following attitudes:

- Give the other person the benefit of the doubt.

- It's not worth dying for.

- Be patient, you'll get there soon enough.

- It's not a referendum on your self-worth.

- Treat it as a trivial matter.

- Don't compete. Wait for a more courteous driver.

When you combine your ability to react less angrily to hostile drivers with your ability to put it all together, you'll notice that your pleasure in driving increases enormously.

Union gives strength.

—*Aesop*

Does the vigilante have a point? Is there a need for some form of direct community action to ensure responsible driving?

Much as we abhor the vigilante who takes matters into his own hands and acts as police officer, jury, judge, and executioner, there is a kernel of sense in his behavior. Through the ages, community censure has been an extremely effective way to bring about compliance with the community's standards and values. One of the most powerful behavioral influences among the diverse ethnic groups that formed our country were centuries-old traditions that conveyed: We don't do things that way, we do things this way.

Up to this point, we have no such tradition to guide our behavior on the highway. We need to establish that tradition. We need to get together and decide to establish responsible driving behavior on our highways. It is possible to accomplish this. In Switzerland, if a pedestrian crosses a street before the traffic light signals, "Walk," other pedestrians will converge on him, urging compliance with the law.

It's easy to see why we have not formed a tradition of driving responsibly. Automobile driving has been with us only a short time compared to dining together, for example. We know what's expected when we eat together; we have thousands of years of traditions. Not so with driving. And as our culture has evolved, the responsibility for enforcing community values has shifted from the community collectively to delegated representatives of the community, like the police.

Because of this shift, the average citizen-driver feels (and is) less involved in and responsible for enforcing community values. On the contrary, there is a strong antipolice attitude among drivers, reflected in such sayings as "Mind your own business," "It's not my problem," and "Don't be a squealer." While a vigilante may personally try to punish another driver, he is not apt to report that driver to the police so that designated community authorities can evaluate the incident and mete out the appropriate punishment.

This antipolice sentiment echoes the taunt from childhood, "Tattle-tale, tattle-tale." It is equivalent to saying, "Don't tell the grown-ups." Strange as it may seem, most drivers are loath to report even dangerous drivers to the police.

Of course, in fairness to vigilantes and passive bystanders, I should add that there is no convenient methodology for filing a report with the police. This could change if the use of #77 on a cell phone to report nonemergencies to the police becomes more widespread. But right now there is no recognized way to foster a tradition of reporting.

I believe there is a relatively simple and low-cost method of establishing this tradition. I refer to Driver Safety Report Cards. Here's how they would work.

Under this plan, each licensed driver would receive five Driver Safety Report Cards per year from the motor vehicle department of the state issuing the license. One side would have the motor vehicle department's address. The other side would have your driver's license number on one corner, and a brief form enabling you to quickly report an instance of irresponsible driving behavior. To send a report you'd fill out the form, affix a stamp, and drop the card in the mail.

The motor vehicle department would record the information about the reported vehicle. Computers would collate the data monthly, quarterly, or yearly. While the data would have no legal weight, the information collected might be used in a number of ways.

Here is what the form might look like:

Driver Safety Report Card—1999

Date _____

Location _____

Car color/make/license _____

Infractions: Speeding ___ Weaving ___

Tailgating ___ Cutting off ___ Reckless ___

Failure to yield right-of-way _____

Other _____

Here are some suggested uses for the collected data:

- When an auto is reported twenty times— for tailgating, for example—the car owner would be notified of this fact.

- When the same auto is reported thirty times for the same offense, a state police officer would investigate. I predict that the notification and investigation would, in themselves, cause most drivers to modify their behavior.

- A state highway patrolman stopping a car for speeding could check motor vehicle department records through an in-car computer to ascertain whether other instances of irresponsible driving had been reported. The officer might learn, for example, that the same automobile had been reported fifteen times for reckless driving, twelve times for weaving, and eight times for cutting off. He could then question the driver about them.

- A parent might learn from the motor vehicle department that his automobile had been observed speeding twenty times when he had not been driving the car. Thus, he would be alerted to risky driving practices of his teenage child.

- A suspect speeding from the scene of a crime might be reported by several motorists ignorant of the crime but each with a bit of knowledge of the route of the speeder. Police could check Driver Safety Report Cards to identify auto owners for questioning.

- A chronically hostile driver regularly reported for reckless driving and belligerent behavior could be identified and investigated long before he actually assaulted someone.

- An auto might be reported by twenty drivers during one day at various locations extending along one particular highway. Such a dramatic occurrence witnessed by numerous drivers could merit looking into by the police.

- Reports on a particular auto might gradually escalate over a period of months: for example, two in July, five in August, six in September, eight in October, nine in November. This indication of deteriorating driving ability might be due to alcoholism, senility, stress, or encroaching blindness. Investigation before an accident happened would be warranted.

But the benefits of Driver Safety Report Cards extend beyond these specific examples. First, public debate and awareness about them would have the effect of bringing the highways back into the community. Right now, from a psychological standpoint, the highways amount to our Wild West—they are not thought of as part of town. Often, anything goes. Because of driver anonymity we may behave in rude, inconsiderate, and uncivilized ways toward another driver—behavior we wouldn't countenance in ourselves if we were to meet that same person walking down the street, in a store, or in church. The highways are a no-man's-land.

Public discussion about Driver Safety Report Cards would make drivers more aware of possible community censure while driving, and this greater consciousness would result in more responsible driving and fewer accidents.

Second, Driver Safety Report Cards would lessen drivers' feelings of frustration and powerlessness when they witness someone driving dangerously. One report wouldn't make a difference, but if most drivers who observed bad driving were to send in their reports, the careless person could be tracked down. In place of asking helplessly, "What can I do about it?" the witness could file a report, thereby gaining the satisfaction that she had done her part. In my own experience, there have been many occasions when I'd have happily dropped a Driver Safety Report Card in the next mailbox.

Here's an example:

While traveling home in bumper-to-bumper traffic on Connecticut's lovely tree-lined Merritt Parkway, one impatient driver, in a red Mazda, passed me on my right. He went on to pass the car ahead of me on its right, but there encountered a slower-moving vehicle in the right lane. Instead of slowing down, the Mazda abruptly cut in front of the vehicle in front of me, forcing it to slow down to avoid a collision. We continued on for several miles that way, the Mazda driver having risked several lives, including mine, to gain two car lengths.

Driver Safety Report Card—1998

Date <u>August 8, 4:00 P.M.</u>

Location <u>Northbound Merritt near Greenwich</u>

Car color/make/license <u>red Mazda—CT XXX-XXX</u>

Infractions: Speeding __Weaving <u>X</u>

Tailgating __ Cutting off <u>X</u> Reckless <u>X</u>

Failure to yield right-of-way __

Other <u>X — Endangerment</u>

Minor incident? Yes. Potential for disaster? Yes! Will it help to report it? Yes! New research on the brain strongly suggests that the more one reinforces all community values, the fewer major transgressions there will be. That explains why the current police practice in New York City, of arresting and interrogating offenders against minor laws like those against graffiti-painting, urinating in public, and public drinking, have reduced major crime.

We learn from experience, not from words.

Words have import only if experience reinforces them. Otherwise they are mere words, with no grounding in reality. Without consistent reinforcement, the child, the pupil, the citizen, and the driver cannot know whether something is true or not.

A community where minor values are not reinforced will have a high crime rate. A highway where minor laws aren't reinforced will have a high accident rate.

Any new procedure like Driver Safety Report Cards needs to be debated, and potential abuses dealt with in the process of enacting such a suggestion into law. Could someone try to make trouble for a particular person by falsely reporting them? Unlikely, since each report card would have the reporting driver's license number, and the number of cards anyone could send would be limited to five, initially. Attempts to abuse the process would have little chance of success.

Furthermore, since the worst thing that can happen to someone reported a critical number of times is an investigation, no real harm can be done. At this point, we cannot say what will happen after the police investigate, but we can assume they will be guided by the customary rules of evidence.

But if there are no teeth to the idea of Driver Safety Report Cards, how will it make a difference? Behavior becomes modified through community consensus and censure. The buildup of community pressure, the debate, the notification process, and the investigation are teeth enough. After all, you don't have to hit your children to get compliance if you have taught them (and they have learned) to wash their hands before eating.

One way to proceed would be to try Driver Safety Report Cards out for one year on a pilot basis, simply collecting and evaluating the resulting data. Do significant patterns emerge or don't they? Do authorities then discern that such information could be helpful in moving us toward a greater feeling of community?

I believe that we have within our grasp the power to curb highway hostility and its consequences: violence, accidents, injury, illness, and death. I have described how the individual can achieve this for himself, and some of the principles that can be applied to hostility in our culture. Of course, a journey of a thousand miles must begin with a single step. Let us start with new manners for the roads; establishing a tradition there will pave the way for the longer journey.

In one night, while driving from Connecticut to meet my wife's plane at John F. Kennedy International Airport, I witnessed four separate incidents where two vehicles raced past me in hot pursuit of each other, weaving in and out of heavy traffic from the far left lane to the far right lane. Can that kind of thing be stopped? Of course it can, if we all pitch in and help the police by reporting vehicles that are breaking the law and endangering us.

For those of you reading this who want to participate in research that the Larson Institute is conducting, write us requesting five free Driver Safety Report Cards. We need to demonstrate that such a method is practical, that drivers will use the cards, and that we can collect a list of aggressive drivers. The cards are addressed to:

> The Larson Institute
> 108 East Avenue
> Norwalk, CT 06851

Data collected will be used for research only, and will not be turned over to the police. The first step is just to prove that individuals like yourself can use the cards, and that they produce a list of drivers who break the law.

We all must choose: we can either be part of the problem or part of the solution. Which are you?

There is one additional situation in which you may encounter an aggressive driver: right in the front seat next to you—your spouse! What if he or she is the hostile driver? What can you do if your spouse rants and raves about the way other drivers drive, or the stupid design of the highways?

By now you know that certain approaches don't get very far. Asking your partner to slow down may just increase the anger and some of it may get redirected at you, together with justifications for the need to make good time. Requesting a stop to the ranting and raving may also divert some anger toward you, anger complete with self-righteous indignation. After all, your spouse is not the one driving like a dangerous imbecile, the other drivers are!

Simple requests meet with only limited success because your spouse cannot stop doing anything; he or she can only start doing something else. Therefore, getting your partner to change requires suggesting alternatives.

Another reason that your requests for change fail may be bad timing. Before an alternative can even be though of, your mate must be in a mood to consider alternatives. Talking when the battle with other drivers is going on cannot get his or her full attention. Anger prevents a person from considering other options. You must lay the groundwork when he or she can better contemplate options. You don't wait for a fire before telling someone what to do in case of one!

The hostile driver's attitude focuses on dealing with something perceived as a threat. I believe that the basic threat is to his or her self-esteem, for reasons you will know from reading this book. But he or she perceives the threat as a real danger. Suggesting that your spouse experiment with new approaches at that point will place him or her in (perceived) danger of losing the battle. He or she won't want to risk it.

The best time to talk to a spouse about this problem is during a time of peace and harmony between you. Though the subject may be irritating, your mate will be better able to control any irritation since no current threat (the other drivers) exists.

The second best time to talk is the day before going on a drive. This allows your spouse time to reflect on the alternative you've presented.

The third best time occurs just after a journey, when your spouse has calmed down but still has fresh memories of the most recent highway encounters.

Before talking to your mate, make sure you thoroughly understand the concepts put forward in this book. Framing the problem in the way described will greatly enhance your effectiveness. Having conviction about the nature of the problem and conviction about how to solve it will make you sound more confident and believable. The more you believe in what you're suggesting, the more convincing you will be. Merely complaining or nagging won't work.

Another word about timing. Many people are reluctant to choose a harmonious time because they know the hostile driver will get mad. Anytime you challenge another person's beliefs, especially those connected to self-esteem, the person is going to feel angry. That's just the nature of our brains.

You're going to suffer either way. Not speaking about it in the way I'm suggesting means you will continue to suffer during every drive you make with your spouse. Speaking up means you'll face his or her anger more directly, but you make possible a much more enjoyable drive. Your spouse will not be able to maintain his or her present behavior if you're consistent.

After you face the tempest, he or she will probably be in a better mood to hear about driving alternatives.

There is no way out of it. Your spouse will not change without a struggle. If you choose not to struggle, you choose a life of enduring hostility. Your best choice is to pick the time when the odds are on your side, when your spouse is least defensive and most open to consider your wishes and desires. If you plan your campaign well, couch your requests in terms of what you want, and persist, the hostile driver will change.

While a time of harmony may be best for your confrontation, the period just before a journey may be easiest. This could be before a routine short trip, such as grocery shopping, dining out, going to the movies, or visiting friends or relatives. Convincing your mate to change his or her ways for a short journey is not as threatening as a total attitude change.

Here are the strategies to use on hostile drivers for changing each of the five stressful driver attitudes, along with typical arguments you might use to convert them to more pleasurable driving.

Changing the Hostile Driver's Attitude from
"Make Good Time" to "Make Time Good"

"Honey, the next time we drive somewhere, let's plan a more leisurely trip. Instead of trying to get there in twenty minutes, let's allow thirty. That way we can talk together and enjoy each other. I get frightened and annoyed when we rush. I don't like it. You get irritable; you're not as much fun as you used to be. Let's try to get the old days back. I bought a new cassette I know you'll enjoy. Besides, there's something I'd like to talk to you about."

You get the idea. Whatever the response, keep pursuing your campaign to make your time together good. If your partner argues that speed is necessary, don't challenge that assertion directly. Simply point out that it is incompatible with listening to the tape together, conversing, watching scenery, or just enjoying the drive. Nothing can be relished while rushing. Say: "We don't have to rush. I hate rushing." Emphasize, over and over, what the advantages are. Driving together should be enjoyable, not stressful.

*Changing the Hostile Driver's Attitude from
"Being Number One" to Treating Both of You
as Number One Beings*

Since automobile commercials emphasize speed and invite drivers to compete, you will have to exert comparable effort to promote comfort, fun, and pleasure. Keep the car clean and attractive. Buy attractive travel cups, picnic baskets, cassette holders, personal decorations for the dashboard, and irresistible treats. When our children were small, I referred to such treats as "emergency rations." Emergencies were frequently declared!

Here are some more ideas for suggesting to your partner a new way of doing things:

"For our trip tomorrow, let's get the car washed and cleaned inside. I'm going to make sandwiches, and I bought some gum and other treats."

"Let's stop at the drive-in on the way for some doughnuts. I enjoy making our trips fun."

"Do me a favor. Don't be so concerned with racing other cars. That takes away from my comfort and enjoyment."

"I bought a new tape for you—it's one of your favorites."

Good times don't just happen; you've got to make them happen. First-class treatment isn't automatic; you've got to know how it feels, communicate your vision, and campaign to make it a reality.

These first two stressful driver attitudes are the most important ones. When you're successful with these, the next three topics won't come up. However, to bring about the change, all five attitudes may have to be discussed.

Changing the Hostile Driver's Attitude from Blocking to Allowing Other Drivers the Right-of-Way

Review the chapters on the driver with a "Try and Make Me" attitude. Reacquaint yourself with the point of view such a driver will most likely advance for his or her defense. Remember the example of Roy, who felt that he would be a "loser" if he yielded the right-of-way. Being mindful of that, emphasize how much you admire your mate for being courteous. This will help to promote your partner's self-esteem. By minimizing or ignoring any negative qualities while communicating your respect for his or her virtues, you make it easier for him or her to change their point-of-view. Talk about what your partner does right, not what he or she does wrong. Being critical can only increase the bad feelings your partner already has about himself or herself.

Say: "I really admire your courtesy," not "Why don't you learn how to drive?"

Changing the Hostile Driver's Belligerence Toward Other Drivers' "Bad" Driving

Changing "They Shouldn't Be Allowed" takes a greater effort than changing the driver who's trying to make good time. The scornful driver sees faults in others, whereas the driver trying to make good time reacts only when his or her goal is threatened. Knowing that the scorner fights awareness of his own faults, suggesting that he be more tolerant of others will also help your mate to become more tolerant of himself. Suggesting ways in which your time together can be more enjoyable for you allows your mate to move away from self-doubt toward activities that make him feel good.

Arguing about the merits of each fault he sees will get nowhere. Labeling your mate a faultfinder and asking him to stop it—or at least stop referring to it—works better, providing you do so consistently each time it happens and really mean it. If all else fails, and he persists beyond a certain point, you must be prepared to refuse to ride with him.

The most frequent reason people give for not insisting that a scorner change his or her negative attitude is, "I'd be doing it all the time." That's not true. Consistent opposition does work. Consider a child who persists in running across the street without looking. If a parent reprimands him only every fourth time she witnesses it, the behavior is unlikely to change because she tacitly condones the other three times. To motivate the child to change, the aversive conditioning must occur every time the behavior is observed. In addition, the parent needs to go to the street with the child, model the correct behavior, and demonstrate the danger by experiencing a car racing by. It takes that much for the risk to sink in. While your partner is not a child, he or she may not change until it is clear that the alternative is the loss of your companionship.

Changing Your Spouse's Attitude from "Teach 'em a Lesson" to "Leave Punishment to the Police"

Punishing other drivers risks both of your lives. And today, there is a real risk that the other driver may have a gun. On this one, you must put your foot down if you haven't done so before. The ultimate choice you can give your spouse—stop punishing people and have your companionship, or continue this dangerous behavior without you—must be seriously considered. I have treated several hostile people who managed to curb their attitudes when their spouses made this choice clear by refusing to get into the car until they changed. Remember Al, who used to watch two football games simultaneously on two television sets? Afterward, he would be in such a rage because of disappointment with his football teams that his wife refused to ride with him.

He transferred his rage into unsuitable behavior behind the wheel. Because of his wife's refusal to ride with him, he was motivated to learn a relaxation technique, which he employed for twenty minutes after the football games and before driving. It calmed him down enough so that he could be civil with other drivers. It was only then that his wife rejoined him in the car.

Rome wasn't built in a day. A new language cannot be learned in one sitting. But Rome was built and

new languages are learned. Your spouse can learn
new ways, too. But it requires persistence, determination, and the willingness to confront your
spouse. Pick a time when you are both relaxed, then
gently explain that his anger is giving you cause for
concern, because you fear he may either damage
his health or get into a potentially life-threatening
confrontation.

David, a businessman, had commuted safely to Manhattan for eleven years. One day his boss passed him over for a promotion, making it impossible for him to move his family to a better neighborhood. The next day, David slapped his little daughter at breakfast, something he had never done before, and was sideswiped on the way to work as he tried to beat a light.

David took his stress home and then he took it on the road. What is stress? Most doctors define it as the body's internal response to events, causing the outpouring of stress hormones—adrenaline, noradrenaline, and cortisol—into the bloodstream. Medical knowledge and treatment focus on this internal reaction, not on any external event. Each individual has much more power to change the internal response than to alter the external event. David had a lot more control over whether he got angry enough to slap his daughter, or run the light, than over whether he got the promotion.

Many angry drivers are just like David. They get angry before they get in the car. And they get angry easily. They overreact with anger to minor frustrations such as long lines at checkout counters, slow pedestrians, or spouses who forget to do some agreed-upon chore.

Other angry drivers don't show their anger, but they feel it just as much. One of the angriest men I've treated was the sweetest, most soft-spoken man you could hope to meet. Inside, however, he experienced constant vigilante-style anger at other drivers. Off the road, he avoided personal confrontation at all costs, but on the road he felt free to vent his spleen.

Deadly as anger behind the wheel can be in terms of potential accidents, the driver's anger and frustration can also severely affect his health. Persistent and repeated episodes of outrage while driving can, indeed, induce heart attacks. Since 1975, I have interviewed more than one thousand patients with heart attacks at Norwalk Hospital. Eighty percent of them had a long history of violent anger or outrage behind the wheel. The association is clear: a temper outburst (or "in-burst") can lead to coronary thrombosis.

The association between heart attack and rage was first observed at the Friedman Institute in San Francisco. While engaged in a long-term study of the behavioral and psychophysiologic precursors to heart attacks, Dr. Meyer Friedman and his fellow cardiologist Dr. Raymond Rosenman discovered in heart attack patients an "emotional complex" designated by a "behavior pattern of competitiveness, excessive drive, and an enhanced sense of time urgency." They dubbed it "the hurry sickness," and found that this behavior pattern occurred in all aspects of a person's life, including driving.

Ever wonder who originated the terms Type A and Type B? From 1960 to 1969, Friedman and Rosenman embarked on a study of 3,200 men. These men, free of any apparent disease at the beginning of the research, were individually interviewed to see if they had the "hurry sickness." Those who did were identified as Type A, and those who didn't, Type B.

During the eight-year period, the men under

study began having heart attacks, and it was discovered that 75 percent of the victims were men with the "hurry sickness." The Type As had almost three times the frequency of heart attacks as the Type Bs.

In their 1974 book *Type A Behavior and Your Heart*, the researchers identified four key emotions that, when present in an individual, may lead to heart attack: anger, irritation, aggravation, and impatience.

When these emotions are felt long enough, frequently enough, and intensely enough, an individual is apt to have a heart attack, if he is genetically predisposed.

Can these behavior patterns be changed? The Friedman Institute sought to answer this important question, recruiting 862 men who had survived one heart attack. In the research project, the men were divided into two groups. One group attended regular sessions to help them curb their hostility, the other group did not. After three years the number of new heart attacks in each group was tallied. The difference in the recurrence rate was dramatic: those receiving hostility aversion treatment had 44 percent fewer heart attacks than those in the untreated group.

What's more, of those who were engaged in the hostility reduction group, and who had coronary artery bypass following their first heart attack prior to entering the study, 60 percent had fewer new heart attacks than men in the untreated group. In the course of treatment, it became apparent that impatience and temper behind the wheel occurred in most heart attack patients. Treatment techniques were developed to reduce such temperamental outbursts. These proved to be surprisingly effective, and became a regular feature of treatment strategies. The researchers reported their findings in a

1983 report entitled "The Recurrent Coronary Prevention Project."

If the Friedman Institute's stress-reduction
techniques were so effective in curbing anger in
heart-attack-prone individuals, why not use similar
techniques to curb anger on the road for everyone?
Their impressive results inspired me to develop a
one-day program just to reduce anger on the road:
the Larson Driver Attitude Change Seminar.

Other researchers have confirmed the Friedman Institute's findings, most notably Dr. Redford B. Williams, professor of psychiatry and director of The
Behavioral Medicine Research Center at Duke University. In his 1989 book *The Trusting Heart: Great
News about Type A Behavior*, Williams concluded
that "anger has a real biological cost . . . for sub-
jects with high hostility."

In the 1993 book *Anger Kills*, written with his
wife, Dr. Virginia Williams, Williams was able to
state, with even greater authority: "About 20 percent of the general population has levels of hostility
high enough to be dangerous to health. Another 20
percent has very low levels, and the rest fall somewhere in between." My work with angry drivers
confirms that assessment. As I indicated in chapter
6, 20 percent of drivers are so angry that they are
likely to be involved in a road-rage incident.

The third researcher who has contributed heav-
ily to our understanding of the effects of stress on
the heart confirmed the discoveries of Friedman
and Williams. He is Dr. Dean Ornish, and in his
book *Dr. Dean Ornish's Program for Reversing
Heart Disease* he concludes: "In summary, then,
emotional stress can lead to heart disease and other
illnesses. Stress comes not only from what we do,

but how we react to the external world. How we react, in turn, is based on how we perceive ourselves in relation to the world."

It was Dr. Ornish who demonstrated that partially clogged coronary arteries can begin to open, relieving disabling heart symptoms, when a person follows a program of stress reduction, attitudinal change, meditation, increase in the quality of relationships, and a low-fat diet.

The evidence is clear: changing your attitude reduces stress and strain, and changing your attitude behind the wheel not only makes the road a friendlier place for everyone, but reduces your chances of a heart attack or other stress-related illness.

For every minute you are angry you lose sixty seconds of happiness.

—Ralph Waldo Emerson

In 1983, I realized that my driving habits were a risk to my health. Racing to destinations, cursing lackadaisical drivers who slowed my rush, and punishing people who "didn't know how to drive" not only made no sense, it elevated my blood pressure.

Using the methods described in this book, I began changing my attitudes. However, as success followed my efforts, I experienced, inexplicably, terribly sad and lonely feelings. Slowly, memories of my father drifted into my awareness. Twenty-seven years after his death, I grieved anew for him.

Memories of my father intertwine intimately with automobiles. When I was barely able to see over the dashboard, I sat on his lap as he drove.

When I grew older and my reach longer, my father let me "steer" while sitting on his lap. Finally, the day came when he pulled the car over to the side of an isolated country road.

"Okay," he said. "You drive."

My father's way of driving became my way of driving. And as long as I drove his way, I felt that he rode with me. Giving up his way of driving felt sad, as though I were separating myself from him.

"Sorry, Dad," I thought. "I can't go along with you on this one. I need to go my own way."

To keep my connection to my father alive, I reflected on some other memory I could emphasize to replace the memories of fast, sometimes stressful driving. I recalled that when he wasn't trying to make good time, he would relax, sing, and drive at a more leisurely pace. I decided to replace the memory of my father's speeding by one centered on his singing. I wanted the car to be a place that facilitated the recollection of joyful times, not frantic ones. I bought tapes of all my musical favorites: symphonies, marches, vocals, chamber music, country and western, and choral. Different music for different moods.

I chose the singing Dad as my mentor, not the "driven" Dad.

We all have mentors. We all emulate someone when we drive. It may be a father, mother, uncle, aunt, brother, or sister. Or it may be a sports figure, coach, race-car driver, or character in a movie. If the style of driving is injurious or potentially dangerous for us, we can choose to emulate that part which is healthier, as I did, or switch to another mentor.

Actually, I've done both. Besides switching to my singing father, I consciously chose to emulate the calm steadiness of the state trooper or airline pilot who never seems frayed, no matter what the circumstances. I like that feeling. It's much better than the intensity of an Indianapolis 500 driver!

Who is your mentor?

For men growing up in America, athletic coaches, military heroes, and sports idols have been the principal mentors. Listening to the last Super Bowl, I heard, once again, the dictums of the coaching profession:

- Give 100 percent all the time.

- The one that wants it badly enough wins.

- When the going gets tough, the tough get going.

- Winning is everything.

These are terrific motivators for a three-hour sports contest. They are also excellent for specific projects, or where extra effort may mean the difference between success and failure.

However, if a person rigidly applies them to all aspects of life, especially behind the wheel, these beliefs can eventually result in illness. Note the number of football coaches who have had heart attacks or coronary artery bypass operations.

One of the most common scenarios I hear from men with heart attacks is that of nonstop work for weeks or months before it happened:

"We worked night and day for three months straight."

"I worked afternoon and evening shifts six months."

"I accumulated one hundred twenty vacation days in twenty years."

"For the past three years, I've worked fourteen-hour days, and brought work home on weekends."

As your stress increases, your sensory enjoyment diminishes. During the course of a day, a person with low stress levels may range through all five levels of seeing and hearing. But the harder you drive yourself while striving to reach your goals, the more your range of emotional responses narrows. You rarely venture into level four, and never reach level five, where you see and hear with relish and passion. Gradually, through disuse of the neuronal connections required for levels four and five, these connections wither. Eventually you can't get them back.

When you are exerting yourself maximally, giving 100 percent, levels four and five are not attainable. You can't give your full attention to a Mozart flute concerto and speed through traffic at the same time. Our brains offer us polarities; every moment we choose a level of existence somewhere between one and five.

Health means retaining possession of our capability to range from one to five, maintaining full possession of our faculties. Ill health means we lose this ability. This can happen when we remain fixed in an extreme position for too long.

Charles Darwin, who spent his life in exhausting research, lamented, in his fifties, that he could no longer enjoy music, theater, or poetry. Creativity, innovation, and the ability to feel passion, joy, and humor, to relish abstract nuances of meaning and to find peace and contentment when alone—all these are lost as a consequence of unremitting strain and competition.

Health requires balance. This book is about restoring that balance. You cannot be fully alive, experiencing all five levels of the glorious sensory experience available to you, unless you have that balance. You can begin to acquire that balance as you drive your car.

You can drive yourself healthy!

How can you change? It just takes practice. Listen to how Charley did it.

Charley, a highly successful financial adviser, once described a journey he and his wife made to Boston from Fairfield, Connecticut.

"Initially, we had bumper-to-bumper traffic, which made it very difficult to make good time.

Then, just out of Hartford, we ran into the worst traffic jam you ever saw. A tractor-trailer had gone off the road. Once on the Massachusetts Turnpike it was pretty smooth sailing, except for some jerk who tried to cut me off around Worcester. But apart from that, the rest of the trip was all nonevents. We still made it to Boston in three hours."

Nonevents! What were these "nonevents"? Conversations with his wife? Games with his children? Music? Scenery along the turnpike? The gentle ride of his luxury automobile? He made the trip at sensory levels one and two. He was dead to the remainder of his experience.

Charley's limited perceptiveness extended beyond the car. For years his hobby had been surf fishing. Frequently, he rose early in the morning and drove down to the Connecticut shore, where he joined other fishermen casting in the surf for fish. But Charley didn't speak about enjoying himself; he paid attention only to the number and size of his catch and how it stacked up to that of other fishermen.

Despite fishing with the same men for years, he did not know their last names, where they lived, their marital status, if they had children, or anything about them as people. He made no effort to initiate friendships, even to meet anyone off the beach for coffee. All nonevents?

During the year or so that I knew Charley, he changed dramatically. As with many stressed, bright individuals I've worked with, once he applied his intellectual gifts to understanding his stress response, change came rapidly. Now he speaks of his joy watching the sun rise over the sea as he slips into his waders at the Connecticut shore. He loves the salt air, the sound of the gulls, and the beauty of the surf.

That special bonding that men have, the kind I

learned from my father, joke-telling and good-natured teasing, now interest Charley almost as much as catching the biggest fish. He's making friends at get-togethers off the beach. In place of living to work, Charley has begun working to live.

Recently I found this poem. The author is unknown.

> *Yesterday is history.*
> *Tomorrow is a mystery.*
> *Today is a gift.*
> *That's why it's called the present.*

Each automobile journey can be a gift you give yourself and your companions. I'd like to share some poignant memories that may stir some of your own.

Montauk Point: One summer night in Manhattan, I had my first date with the woman who would become my wife. Following a dinner in a French restaurant, we strolled to my car, parked under a streetlight, and embraced and kissed for the first time. We were overcome with rapture. Not wanting the night to end, we decided to travel to Montauk Point at the tip of Long Island to watch the sun come up. Never mind that it was almost midnight, never mind that Montauk was hours away, we wanted to start our journey together, and we wanted to start now.

It was a blissfully unforgettable night. The passion and energy from our new love transported us into some magical surreal state in which the car seemed to drift along in a stream of traffic like a boat on a gentle winding river.

We never made Montauk. Sometime before

dawn we drove into the empty parking lot at the Robert Moses State Park about a quarter of the way to Montauk, found our way to some sand, wrapped ourselves in blankets, and slept joyfully until wakened by the sound of early-morning beachgoers wending their way through the mist to their places along the shore.

I had never known such ecstasy.

Canada: Returning from a skiing vacation in Canada, my wife and I in the front seat, our seven-year-old son and five-year-old daughter in the back, we sang songs together. First came the Big Ten football songs. Next, we tackled some rounds of "Three Blind Mice" and "Row, Row, Row Your Boat." Following that, the oldies "Home on the Range," "Dinah," "Down by the Old Mill Stream," and "Moonlight Bay."

We were all incredibly happy.

Vermont: My four-year-old son with me in the car, just us guys traveling toward Newfane, Vermont, to hunt deer with bow and arrow. Though his arrow had a rubber-tipped suction cup, his excitement while discussing his first "hunt" was contagious. In a scene reminiscent of many with my father, we started off before dawn from our home in Longmeadow, Massachusetts, and as we crossed the Vermont line, lights along the road began to wink off. The sky began to brighten when we stopped for sweet rolls. By the time we reached our destination, a small field at the end of a dirt road a few miles north of Newfane, other hunters had arrived, quietly got their gear together, and stealthily disappeared into the woods.

We soon followed—not so quietly, not so stealthily, but as excited as all of them combined. We stopped to pee, we stopped to eat a Fig Newton, we stopped to discuss the habits of deer, and we stopped to rest.

The "dear" I sought came with me.

Connecticut: Late winter in an empty schoolyard parking lot in Westport, I repeated with my son the memory of what I had first experienced with my father. The inch of new snow that had fallen during the night was just beginning to melt under a bright morning sun as I drove into the lot, stopped the car, and said to my fourteen-year-old youngest son, "Okay. You drive."

I walked around to the passenger side, got in, opened the lid on my cup of coffee, and, as I had done with his brother and sister, coached him as he eased the car into black zigzag tracings over the fresh snow. The morning sun sparkled off the snow-etched trees.

I have many lively memories of motoring in America, driving along lonely and crowded highways not to win a contest, but to enjoy the ride and the pleasure of the company with me. I'm so glad I turned my back on the kind of frenzied driver I used to be, for now I can appreciate and practice what Walt Whitman meant when he wrote:

Afoot and light-hearted I take to the open road,
Healthy, free, the world before me,
The long brown path before me leading wherever I
choose.

Oh, beauty before me, beauty behind me, beauty to the right of me, beauty to the left of me, beauty above me, beauty below me, I'm on the pollen path.

—*Navajo saying*

Lucy, my dinner companion, learning of my interest in highway stress, said to me, "Haven't you noticed that there has been an increase in rudeness and outright nastiness on the highway lately?"

"Perhaps that is so," I replied, "but my own experience is that it has been less."

What I didn't say is that I find it has been practically nonexistent. Now, how do you square Lucy's experience and mine? Are we driving in the same world?

Of course, I know Lucy's world exists; if it didn't I wouldn't have written this book. Sometimes I observe it.

While driving to Philadelphia during the Christmas holiday in 1995 to attend the Brancusi exhibit at the Philadelphia Museum of Art, my wife and I saw a Jeep station wagon careening down the middle lane of the New Jersey Turnpike, embroiled in a battle for supremacy with a sports car. I gave the two vehicles a very wide berth, dropping back from the Jeep, which looked like it might go out of control. But I didn't feel involved with the battle like I used to. I didn't say, "They shouldn't allow them on the road." And while there were probably a hundred examples of nastiness and rudeness during the drive to Philadelphia and back the next day, this was the only one I took any notice of and remember.

One night, going to the airport, I experienced

and was frightened by four incidents of aggressive driving, when each time two cars raced each other and included my car as one of their pylons.

Sometimes I reexperience what Lucy referred to. I step back into the highway world I used to inhabit, the world my father introduced me to. That occurs only when I feel I am going to be late for an important appointment or am very tired near the end of a long journey. Since I usually allow myself 50 percent more time than I think I'm going to need and never drive over two hours at a stretch or four hours a day, I rarely run late or get tired and cross while driving.

Recently, I was driving on the congested, two-lane I-95 coming back from Boston. I was leaving extra distance between myself and the vehicle in front of me, just in case something unexpected happened. Three times a car behind me started to pass me on the right in order to squeeze into that space. Two times I sped up to "close the gap," preventing him from doing so. I had slipped into the "competitive" world, and I wasn't going to let him make a dangerous maneuver. Of course, to do this, I drove too close to the car in front of me and created another dangerous situation. During this time, I stopped hearing the music on my CD. The third time a car began to pass on the right, I kept my attention focused on the music and left room for the car to edge in ahead of me. I listened to the music instead.

The particular world we experience around us depends on which areas of our brains have become activated. There is no "true" reality. All is an individually interpreted reality. We cannot escape from this feature of our basic biological makeup. Our brains, where our decision-making processes are centralized, consist of billions of neurons, each of which either fires or does not fire. None "sorta" fire. Each switch is either "on" or "off." Consequently, what we experience each moment of our lives is the product of millions of either-or synaptic decisions. Each synaptic decision represents our brain's response to an amazing computerlike analysis of the interplay of data coming from our senses, the memory of previous information, experience, and our genetic endowment.

Each neuron doesn't switch on or off entirely by itself. Neurons are in modular groups, each specializing in different sensory inputs along a certain continuum. For example, certain modules register shades of black to white; others sweet to bitter; others loud to soft.

One major continuum that is linked directly to highway stress is trust versus mistrust: Is the person (or situation) friend or foe, safe or dangerous, positive or negative? It's readily apparent that our brains must constantly make a determination along this continuum; we could not survive without it. It's basic, and it supersedes all other brain polarities. While a polarity like "sweet or bitter" is not (except as metaphor) stimulated into action until we put food into our mouths, "trust or mistrust" comes into play whenever we open our eyes and begin our day.

During our earliest stages of life we learn to trust or mistrust, and our parents emphasize what's safe and what's dangerous. We cannot afford not to make this calculation.

If, as the result of such assessment, our brain concludes *mistrust/threat/danger*, stress hormones pour out, mobilizing our vigilance and making us more alert so we can contend with the threat, ready to fight or flee. On the other hand, if our brain concludes *trust/friend/safe*, endorphins pour out, mobilizing our ability to love and embrace.

There you have the two worlds! Whichever

"world" our brain's biological mechanism concludes we are facing at any given moment . . . that's
the one we're living in.

To begin driving in another world, one good place
to start is at the car wash. It always works for me.
Before going on a spring vacation, I get everything
in order: I pay my bills, bring my business up to
date, clean my desk, and then I wash my car. That
way, it will be waiting to welcome me when I get
back.

My car, grimy from winter's salt and dirt; full
of papers, some important, some trash, tossed here
and there in the backseat; and with a film of dust
layering the windows and dashboard, causes me to
feel ashamed for the neglect I display so publicly.
At the car wash, I hastily clear out the backseat and
watch as the sand-filled floors are vacuumed. Next,
I watch with pleasure as my car, pulled along the
conveyor, gets soaped, scrubbed, and washed, before emerging.

Four men swarm over, around, and through my
car, rubbing, wiping, dusting, spraying, and drying,
earning my gratitude and tip. I begin to feel a sense
of pride and enjoyment as I slip behind the wheel.
Pulling out into the street, I notice a wonderful me-
lodic, rhythmical hum to the engine that wasn't
there when I drove in. I also marvel at the marked
increase in the ease of turning the wheel and the
smoothness of handling. Did they grease it, change
the oil, and tune it up unbeknownst to me, somewhere along that conveyor?

The day seems brighter, too. I see clearly
through my sparkling windows, and admire the
smart green hood and its graceful lines. The ride is
exceptional, better than I remember it being just
fifteen minutes before, and the stylish dashboard

and soft leather seats delight my senses of sight and smell. Is this the same car I drove in with, or has mine been magically returned to its "new car" state?

Even more amazingly, ·I feel calmer and more patient. I drive with greater confidence. Moreover, the traffic flows in a more orderly fashion. As I wait for cars to clear so I can make a left turn, I notice how courteous other drivers have become!

What happened in that car wash? The answer is simple, yet profound: My mood changed. That's an endorphin high.

What makes the car wash experience so amazing and illuminating is the short time it takes for such a dramatic shift in perception to occur. Moreover, nothing was done directly to me, the driver. I merely saw something happen, and that was enough to markedly alter how I perceived reality. The world didn't change, I did.

In fifteen minutes I became less irritable and less stressed. The car wash experience suggests that if I could find a way to change my mood, I could change the way events affect me.

My mood change at the car wash happened without conscious effort on my part. That distinguishes the endorphin high from the adrenaline high. Adrenaline highs require concentrated effort to win; endorphin highs require a mindful openness to experience—sensations such as seeing and hearing. You can make a conscious effort to give yourself experiences that enrich your life and improve your self-esteem when you drive. Instead of trying to win competitions, you can treat yourself royally as a number one being. Here are some suggestions for enhancing your driving experience:

1. Drive to maximize sensory awareness.
Remember the Highway Uncertainty Prin-

ciple: The more you speed, the less you experience where you are; the more you
experience where you are, the slower you
go. Find the optimum speed that allows
you to reach your objective without sacri-
ficing sensation.

2. Treat yourself to beautiful and/or stim-
ulating sounds. Tune in to the radio stations; take advantage of the varied fare
available on tape, from Garrison Keillor to
poetry.

3. Experience the fun of driving with companions. I particularly enjoy setting off on
a one- or two-hour journey with my wife
or a good friend. Nothing will interrupt us
from enjoying the scenery or our conversation. If I race or compete I cannot fully
attend to the conversation, or experience
the pleasure and affection I feel as the di-
alogue ranges through many moods and
ideas.

4. Stock some tasty goodies in the car,
such as gum or candy. Most cars have
trays for drinks. Sipping a cup of coffee
invites a more leisurely ambiance, and the
taste sensation causes you to be more
aware of other sensations, too, like hearing, seeing, and smelling. Your mind
moves away from preoccupation with competing toward appreciation of the immedi-
ate benefits of being alive.

5. Keep a cassette recorder near you.
When you drive with this new attitude,
new ideas frequently will pop into your

head. Your creative mind churns them out, and if not recorded they may fade.

By shifting your attention from competing to relishing and improving the quality of your life, you will increase your self-esteem, not through "earning it" by winning some made-up competition, but through experiencing a feeling of well-being by attending to those activities that make life a pleasure. You can choose to create another driving world for yourself and your passengers. But start at the car wash.

You may find that you go back and forth between these two worlds—seeing the world and the people in it in a negative dog-eat-dog light, or seeing the world in a positive light, full of wonderful, joyful, and pleasurable experiences with compassionate people like yourself.

The choice is yours. Remember Thorton Wilder's concluding words in his book *The Bridge of San Luis Rey*:

There is the land of the living and the land of the dead, and the bridge is love.

One month after reading this book and memorizing and practicing the new beliefs, it is time to complete the Larson Driver Stress Profile again.

As when you took it the first time, answer each statement as honestly as you can, scoring each statement as follows:

3   If it's true for you, even for a moment, almost every time your drive

2   If it's true for you, even for a moment, often when you drive

1   If it's true for you only once in a while

0   If it's never true for you

Larson Driver Stress Profile

I. Anger

1.	Get angry at drivers	____
2.	Get angry at fast drivers	____
3.	Get angry at slow drivers	____
4.	Get angry when cut off	____
5.	Get angry at malfunctioning stoplights	____
6.	Get angry at traffic jams	____
7.	Spouse or friends tell you to calm down	____
8.	Get angry at tailgaters	____
9.	Get angry at your passengers	____
10.	Get angry when a multilane highway narrows	____
	Total I	____

II. Impatience

1. Impatient waiting for passengers to get in	____
2. Impatient in traffic jams	____
3. Impatient at stoplights	____
4. Impatient waiting in lines (car wash, bank)	____
5. Impatient waiting for parking space	____
6. As passenger, impatient with driver	____
7. Impatient when car ahead slows down	____
8. Impatient if behind schedule on a trip	____
9. Impatient driving in far right, slow lane	____
10. Impatient with pedestrians crossing street	____
Total II	____

III. Competing

1. Compete with another car	____
2. Compete with yourself (to break travel time, etc.)	____
3. Personalize the competition with another driver	____
4. Challenge other drivers (initiate the competition)	____
5. Race other drivers on thruways	____
6. Compete with cars in tollbooth lines	____
7. Compete with cars in traffic jams (to move up faster)	____
8. Compete with drivers who challenge you	____
9. Compete with yourself or others to amuse yourself when bored	____
10. Drag-race adjacent car at stoplights	____
Total III	____

IV. Punishing ("Teach them a lesson," "Pay them back.")

1. "Punish" bad drivers	____
2. Complain to passengers about other drivers	____

3.	Curse at other drivers	___
4.	Make obscene gestures	___
5.	Block tailgaters who want to pass	___
6.	Block cars trying to change lanes	___
7.	Tailgate cars that won't yield to you	___
8.	Brake suddenly to send a message to tailgater	___
9.	Use high beams to punish drivers who won't pull over	___
10.	Seek to damage another's car or person	___
	Total IV	___
	Total of I, II, III, IV	___

Significance of your score:

I. Anger   (possible score: 30)
    High   9+
    Moderate   5–8
    Low   0–4

II. Impatience   (possible score: 30)
     High   9+
     Moderate   5–8
     Low   0–4

III. Competing   (possible score: 30)
      High   9+
      Moderate   5–8
      Low   0–4

IV. Punishing   (possible score: 30)
     High   9+
     Moderate   5–8
     Low   0–4

     Total   (possible score: 120)
     High   35+
     Moderate   16–34
     Low   0–15

Compare your score on each of the four sections and your total score to the range of scores listed above. Then compare your score from chapter 3 with your current score.

If you've answered honestly both times, you should see a lower score this time. One month after participating in the seminar or carefully reading and following the book, most drivers reduce their initial scores by 50 percent. If you reduced your score by an average amount, you are now 50 percent less likely to be injured or killed in an accident where aggressive driving is a factor. You are also 50 percent less likely to compromise your health with a stress-related illness.

Congratulations!